HARVEST FROM HEARTACHE

About the Author

Originally trained as a teacher, Gail Chamberlain has become an inspirational, skilled and honest communicator. As a well-respected pastor of a thriving church in Kingswinford in the West Midlands, Gail works alongside her husband Paul, the senior pastor. They established Calvary Church over two decades ago, in the midst of their son's illness. Gail and Paul have been happily married for over 30 years and have two wonderful grown-up children, Adam and Bethany.

Harvest
from
Heartache

GAIL CHAMBERLAIN

KINGSWAY PUBLICATIONS
EASTBOURNE

ISBN 1 84291 258 5
13–ISBN 978–1–842912–58–4

Cover designed by CCD (www.ccdgroup.co.uk)

01 02 03 04 05 06 07 08 Printing/Year 10 09 08 07 06

Published by
KINGSWAY COMMUNICATIONS LTD
Lottbridge Drove, Eastbourne BN23 6NT, England.
Email: books@kingsway.co.uk

Printed in the USA

Dedicated to the memory of our precious son
Matthew

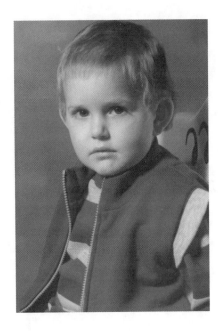

Note from the Author

This is an account of the treatment of my son
Matthew after his diagnosis in 1983 with leukaemia.
Obviously, many aspects of treatment have changed
since: for example, radiation to the brain was once standard
but is now reserved for children with a high risk of treatment failing. The current UK clinical trial for treatment of
children with Acute Lymphoblastic Leukaemia (UKALL2003)
is specifically designed to ensure that all children receive
the optimal amount of treatment so that no child experiences avoidable side-effects of treatment and no child has
their chance of survival compromised by receiving treatment which is less intensive than they require.

Every child's and every family's experience of a grave
illness is unique but, hopefully, this account of Matthew's
illness and of our experience as a family will be helpful to
others; the abiding message should be one of hope for the
future.

Contents

Acknowledgements

First of all I want to thank Fiona Castle for creating an opportunity for this book to be written by recommending me to Kingsway Publications. I want to express my gratitude to Richard Herkes, Publishing Director of Kingsway Publications, for having confidence in my writing abilities. To my personal editor, Carolyn Owen, also of Kingsway Publications, I want to extend my appreciation for the sensitivity with which she edited this book. My thanks are also offered to all others at Kingsway Publications for giving me this opportunity of a lifetime.

A big 'thank you' goes to my friend Sharon Sedgwick, for her honesty and commitment to this book. My gratitude is extended to Gemma Perkins for offering her digital photographical skills. I also want to thank many friends who read excerpts of the book and gave their candid opinions.

I want to take this opportunity of paying tribute to the doctors, nurses, social workers and indeed the whole of the staff, both past and present, of the Birmingham Children's Hospital. Special thanks go to the oncology department and, in particular, Professor Jillian Mann, Emeritus Consultant Paediatric Oncologist – a more devoted and sympathetic doctor I have yet to find. She is a woman who has dedicated her whole life to fighting this horrendous disease and saving children's lives.

I am indebted to friends who supported us through very difficult, dark days and very thankful for new friends who never knew Matthew, but whose lives have been enriched by his story.

In a way, I wish family members who are no longer with us, my mom, my father-in-law and my mother-in-law, could be here to read this book, but they're actually with the one whose story it is. No greater love or support could have been given. I want to thank the sole survivor of that group of people, my dad, for his love and devotion to me; those emotions are reciprocated.

To Adam, our first-born child, I offer my eternal, unconditional love. I am so thankful for the little boy who grew up to be a man of outstanding character, of whom I am so very proud. I also want to thank Debbie for making my son very happy; I couldn't have chosen a better daughter-in-law.

No words can express the love I feel for my daughter Bethany. She has been God's special healing balm for my life as I have watched her mature into a beautiful young woman; our joy was complete the day she was born.

My acknowledgements would be incomplete without recognising Paul, my wonderful husband. I shall be for ever grateful to him for the children to which we have given life and for the years spent with this amazing man. The joys and the sorrows we have shared have only deepened my love for him.

Foreword

The moment I heard Gail movingly recounting her story, I was convinced there was a book in the making. Hers was a story that needed to be told. I am so glad that this has now happened.

Many people struggle with heartaches, tragedies and loss in their lives. It is often a time of great isolation and loneliness. Only a person who has experienced similar circumstances, who can identify with the pain, can really bring comfort and consolation.

Gail's story, so sensitively told, will not only help those immediately touched by such tragedies, but the families and friends too, as she gently explains their emotions and reactions.

The story takes us on a journey from the birth of her two much-wanted and much-loved children, through the discovery, at a very early age, of her younger son's life-threatening illness and subsequent treatment. She tells of the range of emotions and the rollercoaster ride of hopes raised and hopes dashed that she and her husband and family faced through these times.

It makes compelling reading from the first page and I am sure it will bring tears to the eyes of even the most hardened reader. It is a story beautifully and honestly told of a short life that had, and continues to have, a profound and lasting effect on many other lives.

Fiona Castle

1

My Perfect World Begins to Crumble

My world was almost perfect. I had a wonderful, caring husband who loved me very much and whose love was reciprocated. That love had produced two healthy boys: Adam who was four and a half, and Matthew who was 19 months old. Our parents, all of whom lived close by, were extremely supportive, and willing to baby-sit at the drop of a hat. In fact, we had to make sure they had equal 'sitting rights'. Our home was a three-bedroomed detached house on the edge of the West Midlands conurbation, right in the heart of the UK. From our back garden, the green fields stretched on and on, as far as the eye could see. Many were tree-lined, which in autumn displayed the most wonderful colours imaginable. Dotted around in the distance was the odd village, sheltering in the hollows of the rounded hills. What more could I, a young woman of 29, want? I had everything I'd ever wanted. I never dreamed for a moment that within a few short weeks my world would begin to crumble. I was about to embark on one of the most difficult journeys a person could ever travel. Thank God, literally, that I never knew what lay ahead.

I loved my full-time role as wife and mother. The first three years I had devoted to parenting Adam were among the most blessed years of my life; he was a joy to be with. The subsequent 19 months with both my boys were delightful. We packed so many activities in: weekly swimming sessions, toddler groups and visiting friends with children the same age. I treasured these memories and held them close to my heart: I would need them in years to come.

I put my career as a primary school teacher on hold while my children were young, but not once did I regret my decision. However, my profession and my two young children did qualify me to offer a placement to the local college's nursery nursing course. Each Friday of the academic year, Julie would arrive and I would give her practical training in childcare, submitting written reports on her progress and liaising with her college tutor. This was so successful that I was offered a part-time lecturing position, to begin in the September that Adam was starting school. I discussed this with my family and all were in agreement that the time seemed right. Our parents were more than willing to have Matthew one day each week. So I was looking forward to going back to work, but still enjoying my role as a mother.

During that year, Julie was a great help to me, particularly with the swimming sessions. With Adam due to start school in September, I wanted to make the summer special, so we took a trip with her to the local zoo. The last attraction around the zoo was the funfair rides. My boys always liked adventure and so were very excited at the prospect of the rides. Julie went on the rides with them, while I took a photograph of my two lovely boys. Sadly, this would be the last photograph I would have before my world began to fall apart.

July that year was decidedly warm and very often our garden would be ringing with the playful sounds of children. My boys loved to play in the fields that backed onto our garden, but were only allowed to do so once the harvest had been gathered in. Very often they would rush into the house with dirty potatoes or ears of corn that had been left behind. Matthew in particular loved to watch the tractor, and very often the farmer would take him for a ride in it. He would spend hours watching them plant and, later on, harvest their crops. He was so enthralled with life in that field that Paul and I seriously believed he would one day become an agricultural engineer. It was there, in our garden, that I first noticed a difference in him. Neither of my boys made a fuss over things. If they fell down, a cleaning-up procedure and a hug from Mum would be all they needed to put them right. The difference seemed so insignificant at first: a change in his gait. It wasn't exactly a limp, just a slight alteration, but it was enough for me to notice. And there was no apparent reason for it. He hadn't fallen or twisted his ankle. He was extremely agile, but this was beginning to restrict his play. There was something obviously wrong with my son and I had to find out what it was.

The doubts I had had throughout my second pregnancy concerning Matthew's health came flooding back with a vengeance, but apart from when both boys had had measles and been quite poorly, and minor coughs and colds, neither of them had had any other sickness. Dark thoughts crossed my mind and a heaviness of heart began to descend upon me. Perhaps this was what was meant by 'a mother's intuition'. What had my son done? What was wrong with Matthew?

I expected the doctor to send us to the hospital for X-rays, which he did, but nothing conclusive was found. We were told by the doctor at the hospital, 'Keep an eye on him and if he's still not right in a few days' time, take him back to your GP.' Over the next few days there was more deterioration than improvement in Matthew's condition. I found him sitting down more than he was running around and he was seeking far more comfort in his dummy. So I took him back to the doctor and the whole process was repeated with the same results: nothing obvious showing up. Again, we were told, 'Keep an eye on him and any further changes, go back to your GP.' There was still no improvement. In fact, a very strange symptom appeared: the fingers of his left hand began to swell up and he could hardly make a fist. Up to this point, I had begun to wonder whether Matthew had either got into the habit of limping or was trying to get attention. Now I knew there was something medically wrong with him.

This time the paediatric consultant decided that both legs should be X-rayed and blood tests should be taken. We never expected to hear the results we were given. To a non-medical person, like me, human bones have the appearance of a solid mass. However, under the microscope they are pierced with tiny holes, rather like a honeycomb. The pin-pricks in Matthew's tibiae and fibulae – his leg bones – were larger than normal. The blood tests also showed that he was a little anaemic, and together these test results were indicative of the onset of juvenile polyarthritis, or what is more commonly known as Still's disease. Our precious Mattie, as we lovingly called him, was going to be an old man before he was even a teenager. There was no cure, just treatment for the symptoms: a daily dose of 300mg of soluble aspirin and double on really bad days. That was it.

We were asked to bring him back in a few days to see whether there was any improvement in his condition after starting treatment. There was; he was a little more active. Because of this noticeable improvement in his condition, the consultant recommended that we go on holiday to France, as planned, and make the most of it. There was nothing else we could do at this stage.

Paul's thirtieth birthday was the following day, but there were no celebrations that year. The only joy for Paul was in receiving cards and presents from Adam and Matthew, but even these were tinged with sadness. Regardless of the pain he was in, Mattie still took delight in seeing his father's reaction to the gift he had bought him. Our seventh wedding anniversary was the day after, 14th August 1983. Again, there were no celebrations. We spent most of it cuddling Matthew. When he slept, we cried in each other's arms.

We didn't want to go on holiday, but we also had Adam to think about. He had been looking forward to going camping. We didn't know whether we would ever have the chance to do it again as a family, now that Matthew had been diagnosed with a long-term illness, so we had to go for Adam's sake.

The first week of the holiday was spent in Brittany and the second week we went further south, to the Vendee. Adam was so excited; Matthew was so subdued. Adam wanted to race around the campsite; Matthew wanted his pushchair. Adam was so patient with Matthew; Matthew just wanted cuddles off his big brother. We had to watch all of that, knowing that unless God performed a miracle, things would only get worse. The three of us were getting tanned while Matthew was becoming paler. The improvement in his condition was short-lived.

It was at the end of the second week that things took a turn for the worse. We woke up one morning to find that something had happened to Matthew's face. It was as though he had had a stroke, although it was only his face that was affected. We sought out the holiday rep, who immediately took us to a doctor. Fortunately, the rep spoke fluent French and the doctor spoke very good English. He suggested we return home as soon as possible and see our consultant. We did consider the possibility of admitting him to a French hospital, but we somehow knew we had to get him back home. We were due to return the following day anyway, so we kept to our arrangements so that we would be certain of catching a ferry.

We had a long journey ahead of us and it was the August bank holiday weekend, but an overnight stay in Paris broke the journey. Adam wanted to see the Eiffel Tower. I took one final photograph that turned out to be rather foreboding. My husband and boys were stood in the shadow of the Eiffel Tower, while everyone else in the picture was in the sunshine. This was a taste of things to come.

At this exact time, at a hotel in Devon, Paul's mother had an unequivocal urge to pray for us. She knew nothing of the dire situation we were in; we had no mobile phone to contact the family back home. Over the years she had become familiar with what she referred to as 'the voice of God' – not something audible, but more of a firm suggestion impressed upon her heart. So she immediately stopped what she was doing and began to pray for us. There are some things in life that have no logical explanation; this was one of them.

The ferry journey seemed to take an eternity. The countless stares we received from the other passengers were probably the result of Matthew's ghostlike grimace. How could someone, least of all a child, return from holiday and look so ill; unless they were on the verge of becoming a corpse? He had not eaten anything for several days and we had to coax him to take a drink. What little he did have just went through him like water. I realised he almost certainly had gastroenteritis and was probably becoming dehydrated. He was getting worse by the hour.

When we docked at Dover, we drove straight to the doctor's surgery in Dudley; a journey of about 200 miles. Adam was an amazingly patient and caring child. Even though he was only four years old, he knew how poorly his brother was, so he sat next to him and held his hand throughout the whole journey, never asking anything of us, not even 'Are we nearly there yet, Mum?' When our GP saw him, he thought Matthew's condition was symptomatic of his diagnosis. He wrote a referral letter and suggested returning home and taking him to hospital the following morning. His reasoning was that no tests would be done until the next day in any case. In retrospect, I wonder whether he thought he was giving us one last night with our son. This was the first day of September. The summer was truly over and autumn was setting in, but what would it hold for us as a family?

Paul slept, or tried to sleep, in the spare bed, while Matthew slept with me. As I lay there next to him, I gazed at my beautiful son. I could see past the grimace that everyone else saw. I stroked his glistening blond hair. I caressed his once rosy cheeks. I kissed his clammy forehead. The life that had shone from his dark brown eyes was slowly fading away. His healthy aroma was replaced by a sickly smell. This was not happening to my family. This sort of thing only ever happened to other people.

Matthew slept fitfully that night, but I never closed my eyes once. I saw the dawn rise and wondered what the forthcoming day would hold. Was this to be a day that would live with me for ever? Would it be the day that every parent dreads? Only God knew. I wanted to turn back the hands of time. Back to a time less than two years ago, to the day I lay on a hospital delivery bed and held Matthew for the first time. Back to the moment he took his first breath, when all his life lay ahead of him.

*   *   *

I can honestly say I never had any doubts when I was carrying Adam concerning his health. However, my thoughts during my pregnancy with Matthew were somewhat cloudy, although I never shared these with anyone. I deliberated on these anxieties and concluded that I had been influenced, while on holiday, by the presence of a beautiful little Down's syndrome boy at our hotel.

Four weeks later, I was entering hospital for what I thought was an imminent birth. Matthew had other ideas, so the hospital kept me in but sent Paul home for a few hours. I refused any intravenous painkillers. I wanted to be sober while giving birth. I tried gas and air but it made me sick. I walked around the room until I could walk no more. Paul rubbed my back and sang nursery rhymes to me in a desperate attempt to comfort me. I don't know who needed comfort the most: me, Paul or the midwife! It was only during the last hour of labour that I was confined to bed; they almost had to strap me in to keep me there. Memories of a balancing act, three years earlier, were at the forefront of my mind!

After a 24-hour labour, Matthew was born on a Saturday afternoon at 3.00 p.m. It was the 10th October 1981. He was perfectly healthy, weighing in at eight pounds and four ounces, and he seemed almost too pretty to be a boy. I thanked God that all my earlier, private concerns were unfounded. We were delighted with another son. He would be a playmate for Adam. They would grow up together and, hopefully, be best friends. Adam's third birthday was approaching and from now on autumn would be a time of celebration for our family. It crossed my mind that in 18 years' time we could be holding a double celebration: Matthew's eighteenth birthday and Adam's twenty-first birthday. What a party that was going to be!

When Adam arrived to meet his brother for the first time, I was so full of emotion. He bought Matthew a small teddy with his own money and placed it in his cot. Then very gently, he leaned over his cot and kissed him. He showed a gentleness and tenderness way beyond his three years. We placed Matthew in Adam's arms. I remember his first words to his brother: 'Hello, Matthew. I'm your big brother Adam. I'm going to look after you and play with you. I'm going to teach you how to play football. I'm going to be your best friend. We'll grow up together to be like Daddy.'

I was so overjoyed that day. I had my two boys and I was
going to live happily ever after. I thank God that I didn't
know what the future held. Little had I known then that
within a short space of time my idyllic world would be
turned upside down. My worst nightmare would become a
living reality.

*   *   *

This morning I was faced with a different day in hospital
with Matthew, but not one that was to be filled with happi-
ness.

2

It Only Happens to Other People

A few months ago, it had all been a very different picture. Laughter and joy filled our home. I was not only proud of my two boys, but I loved them deeply. Adam was developing a very caring character, while Matthew was becoming more mischievous by the minute. Adam's colouring had changed and he had acquired a rather Mediterranean complexion that complemented his dark hair and almost black eyes. In contrast, Matthew had white-blond hair that was almost contradictory to his tawny complexion. His eyes were not as dark as Adam's but still had a treacly brown pigment to them. They were framed by long, beautiful, dark brown eyelashes; any woman would have been envious of those 'road-sweepers'. His eyes were one of the most alluring features about Matthew. Every time he looked at someone, it was as though he was drawing them into his very soul. He charmed everyone he met, adults and children alike.

Both of our boys were sporty, Matt in particular. He could dribble a football by the age of 16 months! He loved water and was most put out if there was a week when we couldn't go swimming. When Adam outgrew his pedal car he progressed to a go-kart. I can well remember that Matthew's idea of perfection on wheels, however, was his red tractor, complete with trailer, into which he put all sorts of things, legally owned by him or otherwise! Squeals of delight could be heard coming from the back garden and the front of our house as my boys would enjoy the thrill of 'boy racing'. The house was at the top of a small incline, with a very minor road joining it on the right-hand side, about 30 metres past the house. It was here that Adam learned how to do handbrake turns, while Matthew never even bothered about breaking! As mischievous as they were, they never disobeyed me by riding on the road; they always stayed on the pavement. How many pedestrians were paralysed by the sight of these two coming round the corner on four wheels, I will never know. I just have the assurance that they would have had several seconds' warning from the sound of laughter that preceded the sight that followed.

Because of his jubilant personality, Matthew had many friends. The estate we lived on was perfect for bringing up a young family: hardly any traffic; crowds of children of all ages and a profusion of grass areas for the children to play on. But his best friend, who was born six weeks after Matthew, was Andrew, who lived opposite. He loved to play with Matthew, to the exclusion of all others. Almost daily, from the top of his drive, we would hear piercing shouts from Andrew: 'Matthew! Matthew!' Nothing and no one could pacify him, only Matthew. If for some reason Mattie was not in, Andrew would run back down his drive brokenhearted. This was typical of how popular Mattie was.

Even though Matthew was surrounded by so many

friends and had a daily choice as to who he played with, first and foremost he would choose his brother. He nearly always managed to get his own way with Adam. Very often Adam would take the blame for things Matthew had done, and Matthew would let him. Yes, they would argue and bicker, but he always saw Adam as his role model, and what an example he was! They had a friendship that was far deeper than their peers had with their siblings. I don't really know why; perhaps they had to pack a lifetime into a few short years.

* * *

I did not want to move out of my bed that morning. How could my life be so different in just a matter of a few short weeks? Reality was a whole lot different now. I had spent the last hours of darkness with my critically sick son lying in my arms. I was exhausted not only by the trauma of the hasty return to England from camping in France, but with the emotional journey of the last few weeks. I did not want to take Mattie out of my arms. I did not want to face what lay ahead of me. But I had to.

Paul offered to make me some breakfast, but food was the last thing I wanted. I managed to drink some tea, but that was all. Matthew was almost silent, but he asked for his warm Ribena; the problem was that his body couldn't even hold that in. I packed some essentials for both Matthew and myself, as I knew we would be staying at the hospital for some time. As I gently dressed him, I noticed some bruising on his left leg. I couldn't remember him falling or hurting himself. Perhaps I had accidentally knocked him while in bed last night. A bruise was the least of my worries at that moment.

Our GP had advised us to arrive at our local hospital, Wordsley, at about 9.00 a.m. We were there bang on time, having arranged for Adam to spend the day with my mum. We went straight to the children's ward and handed over our referral letter to the nurse at the reception desk. We were then ushered into a side room where Matthew's details were written down. An identity band was put on his wrist and I remember thinking how skeletal his arms were. A nurse took his temperature via a thermometer under his arm, and this alone was enough to exhaust him. By now Matthew was almost white, and he couldn't even attempt a smile. All his joy had vanished and I knew he was really poorly. After the nurse left the room, I lay him down on the bed and gently stroked his face until he fell asleep. The facial paralysis was so severe that nothing on the left side of his face was working; not even his eyelid. He looked so bizarre: he was asleep, but his left eye was open, yet unseeing. By now he was taking far more comfort in his dummies. He had three: one in his mouth; one in his hand, which he continually rolled between his index finger and his thumb; and one that he held in his other hand and rubbed his nose with. Once he was asleep, the two in his hands gently fell from his grasp, but I dared not remove them from his side, because apart from his favourite teddy – Adam's first gift to him – his dummies were the first things he reached out for when he woke.

By midday, we still hadn't been seen by a doctor, and I was getting somewhat concerned. Eventually, a nurse came in to take Matthew's temperature again and I asked when we would be seeing a doctor. She told me she would send the sister in to talk to me. Even though my son was eating nothing and drinking very little, his bowels were still over-active. It was while I was changing his nappy that the sister eventually came in. The sight that greeted her confirmed her suspicions that he was suffering from gastroenteritis. This came as no surprise to us, since we had been dealing with it for almost a week. What I wanted to know was when the doctor was going to see him. We were informed that the ward was very busy that day and there were far more urgent cases than Matthew to be seen first, but mean-while he was being kept in isolation in case he was conta-gious. I kept my mouth shut, but only because I didn't want any more distress for my sick son. The problem was that with the isolation came the omission.

It was sometime during the afternoon that my dad turned up at the hospital. He was working as a courier and his deliveries that Friday gave him chance to drop in at the hospital to see his grandson. He certainly noticed the differ-ence in his condition. The last time he had seen him was before we went to France; I could read the concern on his face, even though he was trying to sound bright and breezy. My father's life had dramatically changed over the last twelve months. From the time I had become a Christian at the age of 15, he had silently observed the changes and development in my character; he had watched to see whether my actions matched my words. During all those years, my lifestyle had spoken to him far more strongly than any words could. It was sometime around the winter of 1982 that he asked Christ to forgive him for being so crit-ical of Christianity, and he invited Jesus to become his personal Friend and Saviour. From that day forward my father's life changed. I had waited nearly 14 years for my prayers to be answered. I believe God was preparing him for what lay ahead. Finally, he had Someone to whom he could turn in times of need, and he would need him because the Rock upon which we had all built our lives was about to stand the biggest storm of all. Dad was the last one in our family to come to faith, and it was as though our spiritual foundation had been completed. He only stayed a few minutes at the hospital, but before he left he asked if he could pray for Matthew. As he prayed, I don't know whether the tears that flowed down my cheeks were for my son or for my father; I never thought I would live to see the day my father openly prayed to his Saviour for the life of his grandson. Those few minutes meant so much to me. I saw a man who had once been an avid atheist praying to the God who had become his Saviour, and he didn't care who heard him.

After he had gone, Paul went to find the sister to ask for a doctor, any doctor, to come and see Matthew. She was not happy with him, but he was insistent. She came in about an hour later with a junior doctor. He opened Matthew's medical records and scanned through, picking up on the diagnosis of juvenile polyarthritis. The sister updated him on his present symptoms and the conclusion they came to was that he was having a relapse and he was to be kept in isolation and observed at regular intervals.

By tea-time, Paul and I were getting extremely concerned about Matthew's deterioration, which no one seemed to notice except us. He was no longer asking for his Ribena and he was silent, except for the cries of pain when anyone, including myself, touched him. Paul went to the sister again and asked to see the consultant who had diagnosed Matthew a few weeks previously; we had seen him on the ward throughout the day, so we knew he was around. She said that the next time he came onto the ward she would speak to him about Matthew. The dilemma of needing to be in two places at once was very real. In normal everyday situations it can be distressing, but in the grave circumstances we found ourselves in, it had become agonising. Our increasing alarm and anxiety was worsened by having to leave Adam with my disabled mum for so long. He was very mature for his age, but with that maturity came an awareness of the dire situation his brother was in. The decision for Paul to go home to Adam and for me to stay at the hospital with Matt seemed the obvious one to take, especially as Paul's parents were travelling back from Devon that evening, unaware of the situation, and he wanted to tell them about Matthew face to face, rather than communicate over the phone.

About half an hour after Paul had left, I saw the consultant who had originally diagnosed Matthew's condition arrive on the ward, so I stood at the door and made my presence felt to the nursing staff. I don't know whether it was the tiresome day she had had, or whether my persistence irritated her, but the sister was more than abrupt when she ushered me back into the isolation room. I couldn't believe the words that were coming out of her mouth: 'Come, come now, Mrs Chamberlain. You have been making a fuss all day. You're acting like a neurotic mother. There are other children on this ward who are seriously ill!'

'How much more seriously ill could a child be? Can't you see how ill my son is?' I screamed back at her.

That was it. I was now fighting for my son's life and she was not going to stop me. I stormed out of the room, down the corridor towards the main ward. At that very same moment, the consultant left the nurses' station and walked down the corridor towards me, obviously on his way home. He side-stepped to allow me to pass, but he was taken aback when I grabbed his tie and demanded he come to see Matthew immediately. I would not take no for an answer. The sister was furious with me, but not as furious as the doctor was with her.

'Why have I not seen this child?' he demanded of her. Then he turned to me and asked, 'How long have you been here?'

'Since 9 o'clock this morning,' I answered tearfully.

He exploded, saying to the sister, 'He is a very poorly little boy. Have you done any tests?'

'Well, a stool sample has been sent for analysis. The junior doctor who attended him this afternoon decided he had gastroenteritis,' the sister replied, embarrassed beyond belief.

The consultant then turned back to me with a remorseful look on his face, saying, 'Your little boy is very poorly, Mrs Chamberlain. I need to examine him and do some blood tests immediately. Do you mind if I take him and do it myself?'

I was struggling to control my emotions; the sheer relief that at last something was being done was overwhelming. No words formed on my lips; I could only manage a nod of the head. He very gently lifted my son out of the bed, took him in his arms and carried him down the corridor to the treatment room. The sister followed; not a word, not even a look came my way. I said nothing. I was just so relieved that someone was doing something for Mattie.

Ten minutes later, the consultant brought Matthew back, laid him in my arms and said sombrely, 'We are having the tests analysed immediately. The consultant haematologist is staying on until the results come through, and so am I. I'll come and see you when we have them. Anything you want, just ask the sister and she'll get me.'

'Thank you, doctor,' was all I could manage. Anger had departed. Fear had arrived. How could this be happening to my beautiful son, my Mattie? What was wrong with him? Things like this didn't happen to us; they only ever happened to other people! All these thoughts were racing through my mind.

I wanted Paul there with me, but I knew Adam needed him, so I decided I would only ring him to come if it was absolutely necessary. When Mattie had fallen asleep in my aching arms, I gently laid him in the bed, pulled the sides up and went to make myself a cup of tea in the parents' room. While I was drinking it by my son's bedside, two nurses came into the room to inform me that the results were through. One of them took me through to see the consultant, while the other one stayed with Matthew.

I can appreciate a little of what a prisoner must feel like when they are about to receive their sentence from the judge. As I entered the room, I was taken aback by the number of people present. They were all very solemn. My heart leapt within my chest, and my mind told me this was serious. I vaguely recall the consultant introducing me to everyone, but the only one who registered with me was the haematologist; a lovely lady, probably around my age. Her countenance was filled with compassion and tears were welling up in her eyes. Doctors don't cry, but she was on the verge of it.

The consultant went on to tell me that upon examination of Matthew they had found not only the obvious conditions of gastroenteritis and a facial bell's palsy, but septicaemia – a potentially fatal blood condition. His liver was also very tender to touch and there were several nodes, or tiny lumps, in and around his glandular areas. Apparently, the bruising on his left leg was of great significance.

I shall never forget the consultant's next few sentences: 'The blood tests have come through and your little boy is seriously ill. We cannot be specific on the diagnosis until further tests have been done. We *hope* he's got leukaemia, but if he hasn't he's only got hours to live. He has got to be transported to Birmingham Children's Hospital immediately by emergency ambulance. You have to go now.'

I was in shock, but I did not burst into tears. I had to be strong for Matt. I had to fight this with every fibre of my being. Something horrendous was attacking my son's body and I was going to do everything I could to help him fight it. An inconsolable, grief-stricken mother was no use at that moment. Those emotions were put on hold for the time being.

'I want to phone my husband. I want him to come with us,' I managed to utter.

'You can certainly phone him, Mrs Chamberlain, but you have to leave immediately. The ambulance is waiting for you outside,' was the consultant's reply.

My insistence came to the forefront: 'I am not leaving this hospital without my husband, Matthew's father! You

have kept us hanging around here all day. Ten minutes is all
I'm asking; you owe me that much.'

How do you phone your husband, the father of your son,
and tell him that his son may be dying? I was concerned
that he had to drive to the hospital – I didn't want anything
else to happen – so I just told him the bare essentials: the
consultant had seen Matthew and had had some tests done;
the results were through and he was very poorly; they
wanted to transfer him immediately to the children's hospital in Birmingham; they had agreed to wait for ten minutes
only, for Paul to get to the hospital. That was all he needed
to know for the time being. I had to bear this burden on my
own for just a little while longer.

Fortunately, we lived less than two miles away from the
hospital, and Paul arrived just as the nurse was carrying
Matthew into the ambulance. He had managed to arrange
baby-sitters for Adam within those ten minutes. The fact
that he had done that and driven to the hospital in such a
short space of time was just amazing. When I saw Paul, a
look of total confusion was written across his face. It was
now 10.30 p.m.; three hours ago he had left his son, poorly
but not desperately ill. What had happened in those few
hours? I dared not tell him any more yet, because he still
had to drive across to Birmingham, a journey of twelve
miles. I hated not sharing everything with him, but I had to
protect him for just a little longer.

The staff suggested that Paul follow the ambulance in his
car, as we would need it in Birmingham. The driver told
him to 'keep on his tail' and to concentrate. We were being
provided with a police escort for the whole journey. Before
we left, I insisted he go into the ambulance to kiss Mattie,

who by this time was drifting into unconsciousness. We hugged and kissed each other, and then I got into the ambulance with Matt and turned to look at Paul. Our eyes met and tears rolled down our cheeks. I could hold back no longer; I cried and cried as they closed the ambulance doors. Paul leapt into the car and pulled away after the ambulance, shadowed by a police motorcyclist. The sound of my weeping was overshadowed by the blare of the sirens. I did not yet fully comprehend that all this was an attempt to save Matthew's life that night.

3

Entering Another World

It was as though I was watching a drama or a movie, sitting on the edge of my seat, wondering whether they would make it to the hospital in time. But I wasn't watching any screen. I was living out the scene. This was reality. This was my life. This was my child. He was lying on a stretcher and I was sat next to him, both of us securely fastened in; the seatbelts essential for the journey we were about to make. It normally took about 40 minutes to drive between the two hospitals, but we did it in less than half that time. Paul drove amazingly well, considering what images must have been flooding his thoughts. He was never more than ten metres behind the ambulance. We drove straight into the Accident and Emergency department where a team of doctors and nursing staff were waiting for us. Paul just left the car and gave the keys to the car park attendant. This really was a race against time for Matthew's life.

It was hospital policy that only staff carried the patients, so Paul and I just followed the nurse who gently cradled Matthew in her arms. With total confusion on his face, Paul asked me, 'Gail, what *is* going on?'

I now had to tell him how seriously ill his son was. I wanted to tell Paul that everything was going to be all right; that Matthew was just tired and needed to sleep; that they would just give him some medicine and we would take him home in the morning – but I couldn't. That wasn't the truth. The truth was very different.

'Oh Paul, I don't know how to tell you this,' I confessed, as we almost ran along the hospital corridors. 'The blood tests have revealed that Matt is seriously ill. They have to do more tests to confirm the diagnosis. They hope he has leukaemia.'

'What do you mean, "They *hope* he has leukaemia"?' Paul questioned in total disbelief.

'Because if it is leukaemia, then he stands a chance of surviving; if it isn't then. . .' I couldn't finish the sentence.

'Why can't he be treated at Wordsley hospital?' Paul continued.

'This is the only place where he stands a chance of surviving. Here, they not only have paediatricians, but those who specialise in . . . cancer treatment,' I said. I had said the word; the word that everyone dreads saying in connection with their loved ones.

With faltering words, Paul continued, 'I just . . . don't believe this. Are they sure?'

'No! That's why more tests have to be done, but they are 90 per cent certain it is leukaemia,' I sobbed in reply.

By this time we had reached the lift. With tear-stained faces we looked at Matt in total disbelief. How could this be happening to our beloved son? Matthew had been quiet all day, but now he was gravely silent. He seemed oblivious to the fact that he was in a different place with a stranger holding him. His eyes were just about open, but nothing seemed to be registering with him.

We were taken up to the third floor and rushed onto the ward. It was as though we had entered another world – a world far removed from the one we had just left; a world where mundane matters were of no importance; a world where nothing seemed to matter, only life itself; a world of cancer victims. These victims were so young: babies, toddlers, children and teenagers. Oh Lord! So many sick children. Even though many were asleep in their beds, I couldn't help noticing how poorly they looked. The intravenous drips to which they were attached appeared to be umbilical cords, offering them life, but the sight that shocked me the most was their bald heads peeping out of the sheets – the most obvious side-effect of the treatment. Our son may possibly soon become one of them.

The sister escorted us to a bed, one of four in a small bay. Two other beds were occupied; one by a pretty little girl who could have been no more than four years old, and the other by a little boy who was a few years older. Neither of these two children had lost their hair, which offered a ray of hope to me, but I was soon to find out that they too were newcomers to this surreal world. Both children were asleep, but both were watched over by a parent. The little boy's father looked at us sorrowfully as the sister drew the curtains around us for privacy; he had obviously walked the path before us.

The young duty doctor immediately came to Matthew's bedside. The attention we received, within five minutes of arriving, was incomparable to that of earlier in the day. However, the consultant from Wordsley hospital had been very thorough in his verbal report to the children's hospital, so this new doctor understood the very basic details of Matthew's case. He then informed us of procedures they were about to perform: blood tests, bone marrow tests and lumbar punctures. Other than the blood tests, they meant nothing to me, but they soon would. I presumed these would be done the following morning, as by now it was well after midnight. I was wrong. Two tests had to be done immediately: a blood test and a bone marrow test. The doctor tried to convey the importance of the immediacy of these tests without creating panic in us. I think he realised that the severity of Matthew's condition hadn't really sunk in yet; we were still in a state of shock. Bone marrow tests were normally done under a general anaesthetic, but there was no anaesthetist available, so it would have to be done under a local. We quickly signed a consent form, unaware of how traumatic this procedure would be. Paul gently lifted Mattie out of his bed and carried him to the treatment room. The sister, who was fully aware of what was involved, advised me to stay behind to give her all the details she needed. Little did I realise she was trying to protect me.

From the bedside, I could hear Matthew's screams and I wanted to run to him, but the sister held my hand and advised me not to. How Paul did what he did, I will never know. He chose to hold Matthew through the whole procedure. A nurse had accompanied them into the treatment room in case Paul couldn't handle it, but he was determined to help his son as much as he could. Matthew was first of all given a local anaesthetic to numb his hip joint; that alone evoked a shriek. The doctor then had to insert a needle-like instrument into his pelvic bone, close to the hip joint. What pain and trauma our child went through we will never know. What I do know is that the screams and shouts I heard that night pierced my very soul. I would have given anything to take Matthew's place, but I couldn't. When they came out of the treatment room, Paul looked as white as Matthew. He has never explained exactly what happened in there.

Paul placed Matthew back in his bed and gently tucked him up; a vain attempt at protection. The sister was still at his bedside and it was obvious she was extremely concerned. During those few hours Mattie had developed a rather strange rash all over his limbs and torso, resembling purplish pinpricks. This symptom alone was a matter of concern to the medics and also seemed to warrant priority. What was happening to Mattie's tiny body? I couldn't protect him from what was happening and I felt totally inadequate. As these thoughts raced through my mind, I heard the sister ask, 'Would you like to see the hospital chaplain? I can call him to come over. Has Matthew been christened? Because if he hasn't, the chaplain could also do that.'

'Why are you asking us that?' I questioned her.

'Matthew is a very poorly little boy. He may not make it through the night. I noticed on his records that you are Christians and I thought it may help,' she added.

'Do you think he is so poorly that he needs the Last Rites?' I asked in bewilderment.

'Well, yes, I do,' was her response.

We fully appreciated where she was coming from, but the suggestion was of no use to us whatsoever. I tried explaining to the sister that we believed in a God who could perform miracles, but if he chose not to restore Matthew to us that night, we knew where our little boy would go, regardless of whether he had been christened or given the Last Rites. We believed, and still do, that until a person reaches the age where they can understand the concept of accepting or rejecting Jesus as God's Son, and as their personal Friend and Saviour, upon death they immediately go to heaven. We only needed one priest and that was Jesus himself. We began to pray audibly that God would intervene in this dire situation and give us back our son. As I looked up through tear-stained eyes, I saw the sister walking away, wiping moisture from her cheeks.

In spite of all the information we had been given over the last few hours, and despite the severity of Matthew's condition, we knew without a shadow of a doubt that Matthew was not going to die that night. We were not lacking understanding, nor were we burying our heads in the sand, and it certainly wasn't purely wishful thinking. We had a strong assurance that Matthew would pull through; we believed God had heard our prayers and was going to answer. Matthew was not going to die that night.

We were now, however, back to the dilemma we had faced a few hours earlier of needing to be in two places at once. A neighbour was baby-sitting Adam for us, but we felt that one of us ought to be there when Adam woke up. It would have been easy to have ignored his needs and just concentrated on Matthew's, but we wanted to protect Adam from the ravages of the knock-on effects of Matthew's illness. We decided that I would stay with Matthew and Paul would go home to Adam, as he was probably the safer driver at that moment in time. He gently kissed Mattie on his forehead and stroked his cheek, then I walked with him to the lift, his strong arm around me, comforting me as best he could. He kissed me, with lips moist from tears, and walked into the lift. As the doors closed, I just stood and sobbed. I was alone now to face one of the darkest nights of my life.

As Paul drove home that night, something happened that had an amazing impact upon him; something that defies all logical explanation. The hospital was close to the Five Ways Island in the centre of Birmingham; he had to go round this and take the Hagley Road West back out of town. Close to the island were the major office blocks of one of the financial quarters of the city. A mile or so further on were some of the major hotels and restaurants that housed and fed some of the employees of those offices during the weekdays. It was somewhere along that mile or so the experience occurred. As soon as he had got into the car and driven away, he had heard himself cry out to God, 'I don't understand what's happening. Where are you, God, in all of this?' Confusion had flooded his mind. What had always been a simple faith to him had now become very complex. His faith was being tested to the limit. Could he trust a loving God with the life of his son? Wait . . . wasn't that what part of his faith was all about: God watching his Son suffer? God did understand after all! In the time it took Paul to drive from the Five Ways Island to the hotels and restaurants, the atmosphere in the car changed from one of absolute and utter devastation to one of total peace and serenity. A divine presence seemed to enter the car and surround Paul. It was as though God answered his desperate cry, literally. He heard no audible words, but this godly presence answered, 'I am here, right beside you. I am with you and I will never

leave you. I will be with you through this trial and I will
uphold you. I will give you strength when you need it and
I will wrap my arms around you when you need comfort.
Trust me! Even though you don't understand, you can only
see part of the picture; I can see the whole canvas of your
life. It is in my hands.'

This was so profound to Paul that he went home and
slept the remainder of that night!

The nursing staff were very good and they provided an
easy chair, a pillow and a blanket for me beside Matthew's
bed; these brought comfort rather than sleep. It was sometime in the early hours of the morning that the blood test
results came through. He was extremely anaemic with an
Hb count – red blood cell count – of only four (a normal
reading for a child his age would be around twelve). The
tests also revealed that he had streptococcal septicaemia –
blood poisoning – which in itself was potentially fatal. His
white cell count was very high, which was indicative of his
body fighting a major infection, but there were also some
'rogue' cells present. However, there was still no conclusive
evidence of the presence of any mature leukaemic cells. The
paralysis on the left side of his face was a Bell's palsy, but
they were unsure as to whether there was any connection
between the symptoms. I was informed that Mattie would
have to have more tests within the next day or so, but they
would be done under general anaesthetic. In the meantime,
they needed to start treatment for the septicaemia, so they
set up an intravenous drip with two bags of medication; one
was a very strong antibiotic and the second was a blood
transfusion. We had learned several months earlier that
Matthew had the same relatively rare blood group as

myself: A rhesus negative. The nurse tried to relieve the discomfort of inserting the cannula into the vein in the back of Matthew's hand by applying a local anaesthetic cream, but it didn't seem to work. This was the first of hundreds of occasions when I had to hold on to Mattie while invasive treatments were administered. The two bags hanging from the intravenous drip stand, snaking into his veins, were his lifeline, his umbilical cord. This would become a regular feature of his treatment.

Paul arrived back at the hospital soon after breakfast. Adam had desperately wanted to see his brother, so Paul had brought him along. He had tried to prepare Adam for the shock he would feel entering this world of very sick children, but no preparation is enough for the impact of the first visit. As soon as their eyes met, a smile appeared on both their faces, even though Matthew's was lop-sided. That started our tears flowing again.

4

The Stark Truth

I had neither slept nor showered for three days. The clothes I wore had been put on two days previously. I had been unable to eat a thing; only tea and coffee had passed my lips. I really needed to get home. It was my turn to leave my sick son behind.

I never realised the air in a city could be so fresh, but anything was better than the smell of sickness in a hospital. It was good to spend a little time with Adam alone; to bring a small taste of normality back into his life. With all the upheaval of the past few days, I had completely forgotten what day it was: the wedding of two of our friends from church, Mike and Sue. All four of us, children included, had been invited. As far as I knew, they were unaware of the recent developments in Matthew's condition; at least I hoped they were. I didn't want anything to spoil their special day. They had to be told, but not yet.

I looked at my watch. Adam and I could still make it to the end of the service or the reception. But was it right? Should I go to this celebration while my son was so poorly in hospital? Adam wanted to see Sue and go to 'the party' afterwards. What should I do?

I decided to go. We made it in time to see them come out of church and we went on to the reception. Paul's father married them, so I knew I would have chance to speak to my in-laws there. Paul had phoned them early in the morning to inform them of recent developments, so it was with very tearful hugs that we embraced. I told many of our friends that day how poorly Mattie was, but Mike and Sue never found out the severity of his condition until after their honeymoon.

I returned to the hospital early evening, leaving Adam with Paul's parents. When I arrived, my parents were sitting with Paul by Matthew's bedside. As soon as we saw each other, all four of us began to cry. My mum came and held me, but her words of consolation fell on deaf ears and my father's loving arms failed to comfort me. My parents were hurting, not only for their grandson, but for their daughter and son-in-law as well.

There had been very little change in Matthew, but his condition did appear to be somewhat more stable. The hospital knew one of us would always be with Matthew, so adequate accommodation was found for us. It served the purpose of providing a sleeping facility on site, even though we never knew who else we would be sharing the room with each night, or what time they would arrive or depart. Many a night I would hear a stranger come in, climb onto the top bunk and cry themselves to sleep. I sometimes felt guilty for not talking to them or trying to comfort them, but I had enough worries and concerns of my own. A time would come when I could help others through their distresses, but it was not then. I needed comfort and there was only One who could give me what I needed. Many people

who find themselves in a similar position shake their fist at
God and run away. I can understand this, but I did the
opposite. I ran to him. I was confused, I didn't understand
what was happening, but that didn't mean that he didn't
know or care. We both wanted to go to our own church on
that first Sunday, so Paul went in the morning and I went
in the evening. It was very difficult to face people and
explain what was happening, but we both felt much better
for having gone.

The antibiotics and blood transfusions perked Mattie up
and he seemed a little improved; again, offering false hope
to us. Those first few days in hospital involved so many consent forms, so many tests, and so much pain and discomfort
for Matthew, but it all had to be done for him to stand any
chance of recovery. We were asked permission for photographs to be taken of Matthew because the presentation of
some of the symptoms was unusual; these later brought a
reality to the written records. By the fourth day, there was
still no conclusive evidence of leukaemia, but everything
was pointing in that direction. One of Matthew's blood
samples had been sent off to a specialised laboratory in
Manchester and it would be several more days before the
results were through.

The oncology consultant, Dr Jillian Mann, was fantastic.
She has dedicated her whole life to treating children with
cancer. She never married, instead making it her life's commitment to fight this horrendous disease. She won many
battles, but not the war. She showed admirable tenderness
when examining her patients and words of compassion
flowed to the parents. On one of her visits, she explained to
us the need for a further test to determine the extent to

which the Bell's palsy was part of the overall picture. They were unsure as to whether its occurrence was coincidental or indicative of something more sinister.

An American paediatric consultant in haematology, the best in his field of work, was at a conference in York that week which Dr Mann was due to attend. She wanted his opinion on Matthew's case and wanted to know if we had any objections to his case being discussed. Objections! How could we object to two top consultants from both sides of the Atlantic discussing Matthew's condition and trying to find a cure for our son? To us, it was as though a higher authority was bringing two super minds together for the sake of our son; and we didn't have to travel thousands of miles to get this treatment – it came to us!

The final diagnostic test was a myelogram, which involved a dye being infused into Matthew's spinal fluid to determine whether there were any strange or unusual blockages. While Mattie was under a general anaesthetic, they decided to perform another bone marrow test and a lumbar puncture in order to see whether there were any leukaemic cells in the bone marrow or the central nervous system. We were warned of the possibility of Matthew having a severe headache as a side-effect of this operation. In order to reduce the chances of this happening, he had to be nursed in an upright position for the next twelve hours. We took it in turns to cradle him in our laps in an upright position and walk with him over our shoulders, all with an IV drip in tow. He was in quite a bit of discomfort, and holding him was not helping the situation, so hours were spent propping him up in his bed while he slept. The results were through the following day and there were no obvious blockages. Thank God! However, we weren't out of the woods yet.

On the Wednesday, six days after arriving at the hospital, I was faced with another awful choice. The next day would not only bring confirmation as to whether or not Matthew had cancer, but it would also be a very significant day for Adam because it was his first day at school. Which child should I be with? I knew Paul was willing to stay with either son, but which one needed their mother the most? Should I stay with my gravely ill son to receive the test results, or should I be with my very healthy, eldest son who was about to experience one of the most significant days in his life; a day he had looked forward to for a long time? Which son should I choose? Paul and I discussed the predicament and came to the same conclusion. It made no difference to Matthew who was with him when the results came through; thank God, he was too young to understand what was happening. But it did make a difference to Adam. Paul had been the parent who had played with him, acted silly with him and watched TV with him – all the things a daddy should do with his son – but it was I who had nursed him, taught him to say his first words, taught him to write his name, taught him to dress himself and to fasten his shoelaces ready for school. So it was decided that I should be with Adam, and Paul should stay with Mattie.

It was an honour to accompany my eldest son on his big day. He was so proud of his new uniform and he insisted he wanted to go to the hospital after school to show Matthew. My boy was so strong, both in physique and character. No one could tell what he had been through in those last few weeks.

After leaving the school gate, I immediately drove across to the hospital. The ward rounds had not begun by the time I arrived, so at least Paul and I would be together when the results came through. Paul quickly went down to the canteen to grab some breakfast while I bathed Mattie. By the time I had finished and Paul was back, ward rounds had begun. The sister told us that Dr Mann would see us last as she wanted to spend some time with us. That sounded rather ominous.

When our turn arrived we were asked to go into the sister's office. The oncology team were in there. Oh Lord! I had been in this position a week ago; I knew what was coming.

Dr Mann asked us to sit down. She then went on to tell us that all the tests were conclusive. Matthew definitely had acute lymphoblastic leukaemia, or ALL as it is commonly known. Mattie had cancer of the blood and bone marrow. They had caught it in the early stages, which was a very good thing. He also had a high white cell count rather than a low one, which again was more advantageous. However, the presence of the Bell's palsy was causing concern. The myelogram was clear, but it would only show solid masses, not cells. The lumbar puncture revealed nothing of any significance, but there could still be cancer cells hiding somewhere in the spinal fluid.

By this stage we were both in a state of shock and the tears were freely flowing, but we knew we had to fight this sickness and be strong for Mattie. So I gathered my thoughts together and asked, 'What are his chances of recovery?'

'The chances of getting him into remission are very high and we would normally say he has a 70 per cent chance of a five-year recovery. However, the presence of the Bell's palsy reduces that to 50 per cent,' was the honest answer we received.

I homed in on the phrase 'five-year recovery', and heard myself questioning, 'What about long-term recovery? What about the rest of his life?'

But there could be no guarantees with this disease and five-year stages were all they would discuss. For the first time reality dawned. Our son might never become a teenager, a man, a father, a grandfather. Up to this moment in time, I had taken life for granted. I was now in a very different position.

Paul's question brought me back to the present moment: 'What treatment will he receive?'

'With your permission, we would like to enter him into the new protocol for the treatment of ALL patients,' was the request placed before us. It was explained to us that new, more advanced treatments were now available which offered a greater chance of remaining in remission.

We gave our permission for Matthew to be put on the UK ALL VIII protocol in schedule A. In other words he would have chemotherapy – a cocktail of highly toxic drugs – and radiotherapy. The chemotherapy would begin with an induction period of a few weeks of intense treatment. Once remission had been achieved, he would then be put on maintenance chemotherapy for at least another two years, maybe three. And all this would start within the hour!

The radiotherapy was somewhat more complicated. It couldn't be given to a child under two years of age, so we had to wait about a month before that could commence. Also a decision had to be made as to the amount he should be given. The normal dosage was 1,800 rads given over ten doses, but the presence of the Bell's palsy complicated this procedure. Both Dr Mann and the American consultant with whom she had spoken the previous week were most concerned. In the whole of their combined experience, they had never come across this presentation in a child who had a high white cell count. They were both highly suspicious of the hidden presence of leukaemic cells in and around the mengines, the membrane between the skull and the brain which links in with the spinal fluid. If this was the case, then he would require a higher dosage of rads: 2,400 administered over twelve sessions. The problem was that in a child so young, it would cause a certain amount of brain damage, possibly around 30 per cent, but if the higher dose wasn't given and there were hidden cells, then a relapse would be a certainty. They were reluctant to make a decision without hearing our comments. I was exhausted with the trauma of having to make so many life-changing choices, but this was the worst one so far. How could we make a choice between killing off 30 per cent of our child's brain and risking a relapse? They gave us 24 hours to think about it.

The team left us in the room to compose ourselves. Never, in my worst nightmares, had I envisaged a day like that. It must be bad enough hearing news like that concerning yourself, your partner or your parents, but when it's your child, the pain is unbelievable, almost unbearable. All you want to do is change places with your child. But you can't. The stark truth had been revealed: Matthew had cancer. He had been on this earth less than two years and he had cancer. How could my baby have cancer? I was angry.

Not with God but with the disease. I was ready to fight this disease with every fibre of my being.

By the time we left the sister's office, my demeanour had changed from that of a shivering wreck to that of a warrior. Our son needed all our sources of strength to survive and he was certainly going to get them. We walked out of the sister's office with our heads held high. We knew the next few years would be a long hard road to travel. The way ahead had already been mapped out; it was not a matter of choice. However, I had a choice as to how I would travel along it: crawling in defeat or marching in battle. There was only one way for me: the latter. We had a battle to fight and we were going out armed with the only weapon we had – our faith!

5

The Long Hard Road

I was due to begin the part-time lecturing job that same week. A few days after Matthew's admittance, I telephoned the college to tell them of my altered circumstances. They were very understanding and gave me leave of absence before I had even started. With the subsequent news of Matthew's diagnosis, there was no way I could even contemplate going back to work, so I telephoned the head of department and explained the situation to her. She was very compassionate and accepted both my apologies and my resignation. I have never once regretted that decision; my son was far more precious than any career.

When we saw the medical team the following morning, we discussed our thoughts about Matthew's radiotherapy treatment. Paul and I had talked and prayed together about what we thought would be best for Matthew, and we had come to the same conclusion: the doctors were the experts and they knew best, so we would go with their decision. We had placed our son's life in both God's hands and theirs; we had to trust them to make the right decision. Before they came to their final conclusion, they wanted the opinion of the senior radiographer at the Queen Elizabeth Hospital in Birmingham, where Matthew would receive his radiotherapy. However, their immediate priority was to get Matthew into remission by the use of chemotherapy; the subsequent radiotherapy would hopefully keep him in it.

Over the next week, Matthew had to have another two general anaesthetics, not for diagnostic purposes this time, but in order for him to receive treatment. Both Paul and I came from non-medical backgrounds, but we soon became familiar with certain medical terminology. When the consultant told us of his drug regime, we soon learned what the procedures would be. Many parts of his small body were injected with toxic medication: intravenous vincristine into the veins in his hands; intramuscular asparaginase into his leg muscles; and, under general anaesthetic, intrathecal methotrexate into his spinal fluid. Thankfully, while he was still attached to the drip – his 'umbilical cord' – the treatment was a little less invasive, as both the intravenous drugs and the general anaesthetics could be administered via the cannula into the back of his hand. As well as all of these, he was still having intravenous antibiotics and blood transfusions for the septicaemia. How his tiny body tolerated such toxic drugs I will never know.

He was also prescribed prednisone, a steroid that came in tablet form. At that time his dose was six tablets a day, taken in one dose. It was a daily battle to get Matthew to swallow these pills. They had an unpleasant taste and their texture seemed to intensify the soreness in his mouth, but we knew he had to take them; they were crucial to his recovery. At first he would refuse to open his mouth and when he eventually did, we popped the pills in, but then he would refuse to swallow and the coating would melt in his mouth and cause him more pain. He would then heave and the pill would end up in a sick bowl: a chance of life wasted. It was so hard not to shout at him for his reaction. He was too young to understand how imperative it was for him to swallow these tablets. Some days the battle to get him to take his medication seemed too much for him to bear. We really didn't know how we were going to cope with two or three years of this, and cried out to God to help us, not expecting an immediate answer.

Later that day, a new nurse came onto the ward. Whether she had just returned from holiday, or was transferred from another hospital, or was a 'bank' nurse, I don't know, but as far as we were concerned she was sent from heaven. She suggested that we put all six tablets onto a metal spoon, get another spoon and grind them down, keeping the powder still on the spoon. Then she told us to add a drop of Matthew's favourite drink to the spoon and very carefully try and stir the mixture together, making one liquid spoonful instead of six tablets. It worked! For the first time since the start of his treatment, he swallowed his tablets. The problem of the texture was eliminated and the Ribena disguised the taste. From then on, that was the method we used whenever Matthew had to take tablets. We never saw that nurse again. Perhaps she really was an angel in disguise!

After a few days of treatment Matthew's temperature had dropped to around 39°C and he was beginning to ask for a drink rather than us having to encourage him to drink. His favourite ones were blackcurrant juice and strawberry milkshake, both of which he liked warm. However, he was still reluctant to eat, mainly because of mouth ulcers. Nystatin was being injected into his mouth via a syringe, in order to relieve the soreness, but it was distasteful to Matthew, so Paul devised a method to rid him of the taste: a mouthwash of warm strawberry milkshake. Paul taught him how to take a mouthful of milkshake, swish it round his mouth and then swallow it. The only problem was that it became a habit, and every time he had a drink, he would swill it round his mouth before swallowing it. The strange thing was, regardless of a sore mouth, he still sought comfort in his dummy, or rather dummies. Unless there were three within his reach, he would panic. He sucked one, rubbed his nose with one and rolled one between his thumb and forefinger in the hand that wasn't attached to the drip.

After about five days of treatment Matthew began to speak in sentences again rather than pointing or just saying the odd word. To us that was a sign of him beginning to recover. He also wanted to see what was going on in the ward, although he still couldn't walk. So Paul and I took it in turns to take him, drip in tow, into the day room where all the toys were. He didn't have the strength to play with them, but he wanted to watch us do so. He spent hours watching us do puzzles, draw pictures and colour them in, or build houses and cars with Lego. He was delighted when Adam came to visit. Adam was the one who brought laughter back into Mattie's life. When I heard them chuckling together again, I began to weep tears of joy. Laughter truly was the best medicine for Matthew that day.

During those first few weeks in hospital, a few friends came to visit Matthew, but most people didn't know what to say or do. Our parents were of immense help to us. They collected Adam from school and baby-sat for us. When they weren't doing that, they came to the hospital and sat with Mattie while Paul and I went to grab a bite to eat. Those were the only times we were able to spend alone during that period. In the whole of our married life we had never slept apart before, but those weeks were spent with one of us sharing a room with a stranger, while the other slept in our bed – alone.

During Matthew's in-patient care, we formed new friendships, bonding with three other families who had entered this alien world that autumn and who had started the journey on the long hard road to recovery. Two of these families were those who greeted us on the ward that first night: Danielle's family and Michael's family. One night, while making a drink in the parents' room, Michael's father offered to share his meal of meatballs with us – a favourite dish of his home country, Greece. Where else would you get an offer like that? Completing the bay of four patients was Tessa, an 18-month-old, pretty little blonde girl, who was admitted a few days after Matthew. We spent many long hours together talking about our common ground: cancer.

After two weeks of intensive treatment, we were finally told we could take Matthew home but would have to bring him back three times a week for the next two or three weeks for part of his treatment; the rest of his treatment could be administered at home by Paul and myself. To be able to bring Mattie home again was so overwhelming. There were times during those first few days when we wondered whether that would ever happen. Finally, we were a family unit again, living under the same roof; something which,

until recently, we had taken for granted. We were somewhat concerned about how we would cope on our own, but
the ward sister reassured us that we could phone at any
time, day or night, and return if necessary. We had immediate access to the hospital, no longer having to go through
a GP. We felt safe, and our concerns did not materialise at
that stage.

Once Matthew was back in his home surroundings he
seemed much happier. His appetite slowly returned,
favouring savoury food rather than sweet. He had always
watched children's TV, but because he was still unable to
walk without help, it became one of his favourite pastimes.
We amassed quite a collection of children's videos, and *Post-
man Pat* was his favourite. If I wasn't in the room with him
when it was starting, he would call me and shout, 'Dom-
pam Pamp's on, Mummy. You'll miss him.' Then I would
hear him sing the signature tune all the way through. The
words are still engraved on my memory.

My friends Pam, Barbara, Sandra and Mavis helped out a
lot by taking and fetching Adam to and from school. Once
Adam was home, he and Matthew would watch TV
together and play. Even then, Adam was so patient, caring
and kind towards his sick brother. They enjoyed bath-time,
soaking each other and me.

I had never appreciated how hard life could become caring for a sick child. Even bath-time in the hospital had been
a worry. The cannula in the back of Matt's hand had to be
kept dry, and there was always a fear of knocking over the
drip stand and it falling into the bath, along with all the precious medication. Before, I had taken so much for granted
in my own home, in my own bathroom even: the privacy,

the handiness of bubble bath, the presence of familiar bath toys, the freedom of time and the fluffy warm towels on the radiator.

Still, at least we were home now, free from cannula and drip, and back to a semblance of normality. However, all normal family activity tired Mattie out and by about 7.00 p.m. he was ready for his bed. He found comfort there and sleep was not a problem to him. That gave us a little time with Adam; something that was very precious and very necessary.

The insurance company Paul worked for were fantastic during that period. They offered him as much compassionate leave as he wanted. Once Matthew was home, Paul went back to work, which just so happened to be in the centre of Birmingham, two miles away from the children's hospital. This location really would turn out to be a godsend to us.

About a month after the treatment began, we were transferred to the outpatient's department, where Matthew received his non-oral chemotherapy every Tuesday. We had to make sure he had fasted from the Monday evening so that he would be ready for theatre the following morning. We only had one car at that stage, which meant we had to plan every journey. Because Paul's father was a pastor and did not have fixed hours of employment, it was easier for him to help with transport than it was for my father, who was in fixed-hour employment. With his help, and on the odd occasion my dad's, we embarked on a weekly routine. It was necessary to have an early start because the earlier we got to the hospital, the more chance we had of being home before tea-time. Paul and I got up and woke Adam as quietly as possible, so as not to disturb Matthew in the next bedroom. The three of us quickly had breakfast and put it all away before Matthew got up. I then woke Matthew, washed and dressed him and put him straight in the car. Paul drove to the hospital with Matthew, who would very often be crying for a drink. The one thing that would take Mattie's mind off his circumstances was the sight of a road digger or some other large maintenance vehicle that resembled a tractor. Those were the only times that Paul has ever prayed for a maintenance vehicle to be in front of him! In the meantime, Paul's father collected Adam and myself, drove us to school, where I dropped Adam off, and then we continued the journey to the hospital.

Paul registered Matthew and proceeded to haematology, by which time I had usually arrived. No treatment could be given until the results of Matthew's blood tests were through, and this could take as long as two or three hours. If his blood count was low, treatment would be suspended and he would either be sent home or, if the doctors were truly concerned, he would be admitted to the ward. We never knew from one week to the next whether we would be returning home. Thankfully, the times of admittance for Matthew were very few. The biggest problem for him and us was that the café was in the waiting room. Those were very difficult hours to cope with.

The results were given to the consultant and we were ushered through to the doctor's room. Here the weekly verdict was given and the subsequent prescription written out. For the first few months Matthew had to have a weekly general anaesthetic, hence the reason for the fasting. Under the anaesthetic, he had many procedures done: a lumbar puncture, where fluid would be extracted and tested for leukaemic cells, and methotrexate would be injected as a precautionary treatment; a bone marrow test, where a small amount of his marrow would be extracted and tested for the presence of rogue cells; and finally, intravenous vincristine was administered. Mattie was amazing when he came round. He immediately asked for a drink, which the nurses were reluctant to give him for fear of vomiting and choking. However, Mattie always had a way of getting round people, even the nurses. He only had to smile and say 'pease', and that was it: he had it his way. Surprisingly, he was never once sick.

In a strange way, I was grateful for those general anaesthetics, because they took away some of the trauma of administering the medication. The weeks when he didn't have a general anaesthetic were probably more harrowing. Sometimes Paul stayed with me; other times he had to go in to work. It was far more difficult for me when I was on my own. Even though one of our fathers was in the waiting room, I didn't want to put them through this dreadful experience; I wanted to protect them as much as possible, so on those occasions I faced the anguish alone. I had to sit Matthew on my lap and hold his wrist very tightly and very still. The doctor rubbed a local anaesthetic cream on the back of his hand and waited a few moments, trying to distract Matthew from the forthcoming procedure. Matthew soon learned what this meant and so the struggle began. It took all my strength to hold him still while the doctor injected a two-inch needle into the vein in the back of his hand and slowly released the contents of the syringe into his bloodstream. Apparently, it was not only painful inserting the needle, but the medication stung as it surged through his veins. Very often Mattie would scream at the doctor, 'Nasty, horrible man. You hurtin' me!' Never once did Mattie yell or scream at me for taking him into the room or holding him still. He never once blamed me for inflicting pain. For that I will be eternally grateful.

From the treatment room we went to the pharmacy to collect the weekly supply of drugs, and from there to the car park. If Paul stayed, we would take Mattie across to Tesco's café, where he would devour beans on toast, the effects of fasting outweighing those of the anaesthetic!

It was about five weeks into treatment that we received the fantastic news that Matthew was in remission. In other words, all obvious leukaemic cells had been destroyed. I wanted to use the word 'cured', but the doctors very quickly informed me they could not use that word because they could never be certain that there were not some rogue cells hiding somewhere in his body waiting to multiply again.

However, this great news was tinged with sadness, as the reality of the severity of leukaemia also hit us the same day. At the outpatients clinic, we would look out for the families we shared a bay with on the ward; Danielle's, Michael's and Tessa's. We would share news of the week's progress or deterioration, as the case may be. Michael was missing that day, and we learned how suddenly death's grip could get a hold of a child and whisk them away. We felt guilty about going home to celebrate while Michael's parents went home to grieve. The stark truth of leukaemia hit us.

It was only a few days later that my heart sank again. I went into Mattie's bedroom to wake him up, only to find his beautiful blond hair lying in clumps on the pillow. I picked him up in my arms and held him and sobbed my heart out. I wanted to pick up the thousands of strands and put them back where they belonged, but I couldn't. Because it had taken so long to happen, we thought Matt had escaped that particular side-effect of treatment, but he hadn't. We had been warned that it would happen; even so, it was a major shock. His head was like a patchwork quilt of differing thicknesses of hair. Within a few days there were only a few blond wisps left. Because of the onset of colder weather and to reduce embarrassment, we bought Matthew a collection of baseball caps. He grew to love these and they became very much part of his daily attire.

The other major side-effect of the treatment was caused by the steroids; his body became so bloated he looked like a little Michelin man. Both his body and his features had become distorted and he really did not look like my little boy. If I gazed too long at his shell, awful thoughts would cross my mind: 'Where has my little boy gone? Who has taken him from me? Who is this in his place?' But then I would look into the depths of his dark brown eyes and be assured that my little boy was still in that shell somewhere.

Matthew spent his second birthday with just his immediate family. We could not risk any infection at this stage of his treatment, so a party was out of the question. Fortunately, he was not old enough to be disappointed. Adam, however, was a different matter. How could I deprive him, and indeed us, of celebrating his fifth birthday? I couldn't have a party at home with Matthew, but then Matthew would miss out on the celebrations. So many choices had already been made between my two boys and we were faced with yet another one. We decided that on this occasion it was more important for Adam to have the attention. I would go with Adam, and Paul would stay with Matt. The party was held at McDonald's, with a cake made in the shape of a car from one of Adam's favourite TV programmes, *The Dukes of Hazzard*. Many of his friends brought along younger brothers or sisters who were Matthew's friends; it was a major battle that evening to keep my emotions under control, let alone smile and laugh. But I did, for Adam's sake.

It was the 13th October 1983, three days after Matthew's second birthday, that we had our first appointment with the radiographer at the Queen Elizabeth Hospital in Birmingham. The whole of the medical team had made their decision regarding the amount of radiation Matthew should receive. The risk of brain damage outweighed the risk of relapse, so they chose to give him the normal 1,800 rads, over ten consecutive doses. He was going to have radiotherapy to his brain and, in order for it to be administered accurately, a device had to be made to secure his head in place for the treatment. This device was known as a mask and it was made out of clear perspex. It had to be made to measure from a plaster cast. Matthew had to be given a sedative in order for the cast to be taken. We returned a few days later for the fitting and for measurements to be placed exactly where the beams of radiation should be targeted.

His first course started on the 19th October and finished two days after Adam's fifth birthday on the 3rd November. I thought the chemotherapy was traumatic enough, but to me this was worse. Apparently, the radiotherapy itself was pain-free, but the emotional anxiety it caused was dreadful.

We were allowed to take him into the X-ray room and stay with him while preparations were made. We laid him down on the treatment table and his mask was then positioned and bolted down, with Matthew in it, to the table. I had to release his hand as they secured his limbs. The panic and the screams that came from Mattie tore me apart. We then had to walk out of the room, with his squealing pleas of 'Mummy, don't leave me. Daddy, help me. Where are you?' We used a TV intercom to talk to him, but he could never hear us above his screaming. I really have no idea how we all got through the ten sessions.

By December, Matthew had started walking again. He was still ungainly, but nevertheless he could walk unaided. What joy that brought us! He was absolutely delighted on Christmas morning with his main present – a red pedal-tractor with a trailer. He spent the whole of the day riding it around the house with Adam chasing him on his present – a go-kart. We had to move furniture for the racetrack. It was one day of normality and how fantastic that was. Boxing Day brought the usual trip to the clinic, with yet more invasive treatment.

By the start of 1984, Matthew was progressing well. The treatment requiring general anaesthetics, and the steroid tablets, had been reduced to a monthly regime, and the course of intramuscular asparaginase had finished. However, the rest of his treatment remained the same. Matthew's bloated features had almost disappeared and a fine, blond down had begun to appear on his head. Some families at the clinic isolated their children from society for fear of them catching ailments and becoming ill, and I can fully understand their decision, but we chose differently. Life returned to a semblance of normality; Matthew attended toddler group, and trips to the swimming baths resumed.

Matthew remained as an outpatient until May of that year. During one of his routine appointments the doctor decided to order a chest X-ray, as Matt had had rather a bad cold, which had left him with a nasty cough. It revealed a shadow on his lungs, and he was immediately admitted to intensive care, where further tests revealed pneumocystis – a form of pneumonia. We were warned that this was potentially fatal to leukaemic patients and that he would be in hospital for several weeks. Our parents were once again our safety net and helped out in whatever way was needed. They not only prayed themselves but got hundreds of other people to do likewise. Matthew was discharged four days later! What amazed the doctors just as much was that within two weeks his lungs were absolutely clear. Not even scar tissue remained.

When he was well enough, Matthew loved to play with Andrew, his best friend. Since his diagnosis, Andrew had come to our house to play, but by the summer, Margaret, Andrew's mum, felt confident enough for them to play at her house. It was on one such occasion that Mattie fell out of Margaret's patio window and broke his wrist. She was understandably very upset, but it was an accident that could have happened to anyone, and after everything Mattie had been through, a plaster cast was nothing to him. It became more of a weapon than a hindrance!

If these had been the only hurdles that we faced in 1984, then life would have been relatively easy. But they weren't. A greater one was yet to come.

6

Going Round in Circles

After twelve months of treatment, Matthew's progress appeared to be well on track and he was attending the outpatients clinic every fortnight. A lot of pressure was taken off us as a family by not having to make the weekly trips. At times we almost forgot the fact that Matthew was on chemotherapy and I had started to refer to his illness as something in the past rather than the present. He was well enough to celebrate his third birthday with a few friends, although we had to ask them not to come if they had any sign of illness. Mattie chose McDonald's as the venue and a tractor as his birthday cake design. We had a great time, with all the clearing up left for the staff.

With Adam's sixth birthday less than three weeks later, it was not only a busy but an expensive time of year. 'Well, in 15 years' time we can have a joint eighteenth and twenty-first birthday celebration; one great big party!' I thought, as I began to organise and send out Adam's invitations. Once again McDonald's was the chosen venue. This time the cake design was based on Kit, the car from the TV series *Knight Rider*. Of all the children who were invited, Adam was most excited about Matthew coming. I was so glad it was going to be different from the previous year.

Matthew had been a little subdued all day and we thought this was due to Adam receiving most of the attention. Rather than make an issue of it, we chose to ignore his attitude. It was during the party that we realised we had been wrong in our assumptions. He was rather reluctant to join in the games at first, which really was not Matthew since he was a very sociable creature, as indeed was Adam. While all the others were wolfing down their food, Matthew was picking at his, which again was out of character. When the games resumed, he wanted to sit on my lap for a cuddle. I thought perhaps he was tired with all the excitement of the day, but then Paul and I froze at the words Mattie uttered: 'My headie hurts.'

We had been warned, soon after diagnosis, of the tell-tale sign of a relapse. As the months went by and all was going well, these warnings went to the back of our minds. But with that utterance, they came flooding back. Sudden lethargy, headaches and vomiting were the first symptoms. No sooner had we fixed our fearful gaze on each other than our ears heard the awful sound of retching. I felt Mattie lean forward and I looked down to see him vomiting on the floor. I felt like joining him at that moment, but for very different reasons. The McDonald's staff were great and cleared up the mess. Everyone thought he had eaten too much, but we suspected differently. We told our parents, who were at the party, that we would get him checked out at the hospital the next day. We never told them of our fears; we didn't want to worry them unnecessarily.

I didn't sleep a wink that night. Paul refused to speak

about the possibility of a relapse, but I could see in his eyes that he was truly worried. We gave Mattie nothing to eat or drink the next morning because we presumed, rightly so, that they would want to do a lumbar puncture and bone marrow test. They were fantastic on the ward. We didn't have to pre-arrange a consultation; just a phone call warning of our arrival was required. A bed was waiting for Matthew, and one of the doctors examined him upon arrival. His diagnosis was very bleak. He was sure that Matthew either had the early symptoms of meningitis or he was going into relapse; either way, he was a very sick child. Matthew was rushed down to theatre for the diagnostic tests. It would be the next day before we found out the results. I cannot begin to put into words what Paul and I were feeling. We really didn't know which disease we would prefer Mattie to have – not that there was any point in thinking that way, because the choice was not ours to make; the illness, whichever one, had already taken a grip of him. We were into the waiting game again. Paul went home that night to Adam and warned our parents of the possible outcome. I stayed beside Mattie's bed all night, holding a sick bowl for him. Our lovely little boy was so poorly again.

Paul arrived quite early the next morning after dropping Adam off at his grandparents' to watch Saturday morning TV – anything to take his mind off what was happening again. Soon afterwards, our friends Andre and Joy turned up. It was great to see someone other than family; someone for whom we didn't have to be strong. They sat with Matthew while we went down to the cafeteria under the pretext of eating but really wanting to spend time talking through the possibilities of what we were going to face in the next few hours.

We were only gone about half an hour, but during that time the results had come through and the doctors were looking for us. We were taken into the sister's office. That office had only brought bad news and I did not want to enter it, but I knew I must. Paul put his arm around my waist and ushered me in. As soon as we saw Dr Mann, we knew Mattie was in trouble. Usually she only saw new patients and those who had relapsed. With a serious countenance, she asked us to sit down. I wanted to put my hands over my ears; I did not want to hear what she was about to say. I was hoping beyond reason that if I didn't hear it, then it wouldn't be true. But I just did as I was told, obeying like a robot. In a judicial trial, the condemned man stands for his sentence; we sat.

She told us that Matthew had had a relapse; the leukaemia had returned. Fortunately it wasn't a total relapse, as both his blood and his bone marrow were clear, but there was a profusion of leukaemic cells in his spinal fluid. He had had a CNS – central nervous system – relapse.

'No! Not again!' I cried out. Our little boy had been through enough. 'Oh God, not again!' I lamented.

I stood up and walked to the window, not wanting to hear any more. I wanted to be out there in the normal world, with my little three-year-old boy, a boy who was healthy, but I couldn't be. I had to be in this room, with these specialists, listening to their recommendations for renewing his programme of treatment.

Their plan of action was to follow that of the UK ALL VIII for meningial relapse: a two-week course of intensive induction treatment, similar to before, followed by three years of maintenance chemotherapy. He would have to have another bout of radiotherapy, but this time it would be the higher dose. Straightaway, I understood what all this meant. To go through it initially is bad enough, but when you know what is coming, it is far worse.

'What about a bone marrow transplant?' I heard Paul ask.

'I'm very sorry, but it's out of the question,' Dr Mann replied. She went on to explain, as we understood it, that it was going to be harder to get him into remission. A bone marrow transplant was only possible if the patient was in remission; Mattie needed radiotherapy as soon as possible to achieve this. Because of his size, he couldn't have both immediate, localised radiotherapy and later total body radiotherapy, which was a major part of the treatment required for a bone marrow transplant. His tiny body wouldn't tolerate this amount; it would kill him. The next dose of radiotherapy would have to last him a lifetime. This was going to be his last chance of any long-term recovery.

We also recognised that the intended higher dose of radiotherapy would definitely cause about 30 per cent brain damage. There was an attempt by the doctor to lessen the setback by pointing out the fact that Matthew was well above average intelligence, so it would bring him down to average or just below. However, this appeared to be the least of their worries. Because he was now three years old, the radiotherapy did not have to be delayed, but the chemotherapy induction had to be given first, starting immediately.

We were in a state of shock as we walked out of the sister's office. We couldn't face Matt or Andre and Joy until we had taken some time to compose ourselves. We went into the parents' room and just fell into each other's arms and wept. There were a few other parents in the room, but they soon gave us privacy; no explanation was required. They knew the reason for the tears. They had been there themselves.

'Oh God, how can this happen again? How can Mattie go through all that again? If ever there was a time I needed you, Jesus, it's now,' I implored. 'We cannot do this again in our own strength; none of us can.' I wanted God to wave a magic wand and wipe it all away, but that wasn't going to happen. We were going to have to start out on the long hard road once again and the first step was to go back to Mattie's bedside, not with tears streaming down our cheeks, but with a warrior spirit once more to fight the giant, cancer.

Mattie lost his hair much sooner into treatment this time. It had already gone by the time he had his first radiotherapy appointment. A double mask had to be made this time, which covered both sides of his head. When the mask was first placed on Mattie, it obviously brought back horrendous memories for him. To lessen the impact, we tried to convince him that he was one of the characters from *Star Wars: The Return of the Jedi*. We suggested that he was R2D2, C3PO or even Darth Vader himself. We tried to help him imagine that the treatment table was the Millennium Falcon spaceship from the film – anything to reduce the emotional trauma of the previous sessions. It appeared to work – until the first session started. This time round, Mattie was stripped naked and his double mask was positioned and bolted face down, with Mattie in it, on the table. Not only did his head have to receive this aggressive treatment, but also the whole of his spine. I felt evil allowing my son to be put through such an ordeal, but as far as the medical world was concerned, it was his final chance. How could I deprive him of that?

The first of his twelve treatment sessions was on the 11th December 1984. After it we were asked to stay behind, as the radiographer wanted to speak to us before we left. With everything we had been through, nothing could prepare us for the next blow we were about to receive. He explained that the measurements that had been drawn up on Mattie's mask were incorrect by a fraction of a millimetre and as a result, it was highly likely that the radiotherapy he had just received had blinded him. The mistake would be corrected immediately, but any damage would be irreversible. How do you respond to something like that without the consequences being a life sentence? We just had to walk away without uttering a word.

I decided to drive home, while Paul sat in the back with Matthew: a reversal of what we usually did, and a mistake. My mind was clearly not on the road that afternoon and I was driving along a dual carriageway, slowing up for the traffic queue ahead, when a motorcyclist came out of a side road, across my path. I didn't brake quickly enough, and collided with him. He stared at me as he hit the windscreen, both of us in a state of disbelief. He rolled off the car bonnet and disappeared, I presumed, under the car. I leapt out of the car expecting to see a bloody corpse. Instead, I saw a rather shocked young man, who got up off the floor, picked up his mangled bike and started to walk away, apologising! I offered my apologies, suggested that it wasn't a good idea to go anywhere other than the hospital and volunteered to take him there. He rejected my offer and was very eager to depart the scene. It wasn't until I turned round that I understood the profuse apology and the hasty getaway. I had forgotten that we operated the child locks in the back of the car. Paul couldn't unlock the car door to get out and he was frantically screaming and shouting at me to let him out. The poor guy thought he was yelling at him for damaging the car. By the time I released Paul, the young man in question was making his frantic escape, albeit with a limp and a twisted wreck of a motorbike. If the surrounding circumstances hadn't been so serious, it would have been one of those side-splitting moments in time. On a more serious note, I will never understand how the young man wasn't killed outright. To me it was a miracle.

Another miracle occurred the following day: it became clear that Matthew's eyes had not been affected by the miscalculation; he had escaped blindness by a fraction of a millimetre. We still had eleven more sessions to go and we realised that Christmas would be in the middle of it all.

We were more than halfway through the course when yet another hurdle blocked our path. During all these months of treatment, we had continued to attend church two or three times each week, and in addition Paul and I ran the youth department. Matthew used to enjoy going to church when he was well enough and loved to sing, his favourite song being 'Ah Lord God, Thou hast made the heavens'. He would sing the chorus with gusto: 'Nothing, nothing, absolutely nothing, nothing is impossible with Thee.' He had been practising singing 'Away in a manger' for weeks and was greatly disappointed that he could not go to the carol service on the Sunday before Christmas. Paul was due to play the guitar, so I had to stay at home with

Matthew, while Adam went with his dad. About half an hour after they left for church, Mattie fell off the bottom step of the stairs and was in agony; I had to phone for Paul to come home. We took him to the local hospital, where an X-ray was taken. It revealed a greenstick fracture of his left ankle. He was put in a temporary plaster cast overnight and we had to return the following day for a permanent cast.

The following day, Monday, happened to be Christmas Eve and the oncology clinic had been moved forward a day. It would have been too risky for many of the children, including Matthew, to have missed their weekly examination. Christmas Eve for us that year began with a whistle-stop visit to the haematology department of the Birmingham Children's Hospital followed by radiotherapy treatment at the Queen Elizabeth Hospital. We returned to the children's hospital for Matthew's results and subsequent treatment, part of which included the need for a general anaesthetic. From there, we quickly fed him at Tesco's and rushed back to our local hospital – Russell's Hall – for a permanent plaster cast to be put on his broken ankle! Adam had wanted to spend the day with his brother. We had tried to dissuade him from coming along because of the length and intensity of the day, but he had insisted. He reasoned with us, 'Mattie's my brother, and brothers should be together on Christmas Eve, talking about Father Christmas and what he might bring us – if we're good! Mattie's been very good this year and I want to be a good boy. Good boys look after their brothers when they're poorly and try to make them laugh when they're sad. That's what I want to do today, not just because it's Christmas tomorrow, but because I love my brother very much and I want to be with him.'

What could we say in reply, other than a tearful 'OK'?

Bob Geldof wrote the theme song for Band Aid that year, to raise money for the starving millions in Africa, but the words to his song 'Do they know it's Christmas?' were so applicable to us as a family that Christmas. Apart from the boys' excitement over their presents, there was little to celebrate that year, even though I have vivid memories of Matthew sitting at his drum kit, trying to play the base drum with his leg in plaster. He actually managed very well. We ended up back at the children's hospital the day after Boxing Day because Matthew had a temperature. They gave him intravenous antibiotics and he also required a blood transfusion. The infusion was completed by 10.00 p.m. and they allowed us to go home because it was Christmas. His radiotherapy sessions had to be put on hold for a few days until he was better, but with that delay, and the omission of treatment on Christmas Day and Boxing Day, he didn't finish the course until New Year's Eve. Paul and I felt the season had just passed us by. There really was no Christmas for us that year. We hoped that the next day – 1st January 1985 – would bring a year of better health for Matthew. Nothing could be worse than the one we had just had, could it?

7

Decision Time

Society had many fears around that time, including the arrival of AIDS. We didn't fully appreciate the implications of what this disease would mean to humanity at that time; even Western society would not be immune to its ravages. Matthew was receiving regular blood transfusions, and screening for HIV had not yet begun; these transfusions were a matter of life or death to him and at that time considerations of future consequences were of little importance when faced with the fragility of life. We will never know what other diseases were unknowingly pumped into Mattie's small body in an attempt to heal it.

By the beginning of 1985, Matthew had been put on maintenance treatment and the frantic pace of life of the previous two months seemed to settle down again. By the late spring we were back into fortnightly visits and began to feel a little more secure.

It was around this time that we really felt impressed to act upon something we, Paul in particular, had experienced two years earlier; something which because of our circumstances should have been forgotten, but it hadn't. In actual fact, it had not only remained, but had become more compelling. A few months before Matthew's initial diagnosis, while on our way to the youth service at our church, we had passed a large group of young people who were gathered on a street corner. Paul had felt at that moment as though God had asked him a question: 'Why are you travelling three miles to church when there is a need on your own doorstep?'

It was not an audible voice he heard, but more an impression that had been placed upon his heart. With all the trauma of Matthew's illness, starting a church was the last thing we would have planned to do. However, we could not escape this 'calling'. We knew it was from God because, despite our circumstances, we couldn't forget it. It just got stronger over the years.

The last thing we wanted to do was tear people away from our church to start another one. The influence we had at that time, particularly with over 70 young people in the youth group, would have caused exactly that. So, in the May of that year, we decided to leave our church in order to make preparations for starting a new church in Kingswinford; we had nowhere to go, so people couldn't follow us. It was difficult, but we severed the ties. However, there were a few exceptions: both sets of parents wanted to support us, as well as another elderly couple, Doug and Margaret. There was one other young married couple who truly felt they should join us: Kevin and Andrea. We asked them to really search their hearts about the matter because it was not going to be an easy task. They could not be swayed in their decision and so joined us; together with Adam and Matthew, we were a group of twelve. We wanted to pioneer a church, somewhere in Kingswinford, but with no building and no money! Naturally speaking, it was a ridiculous thing to do, but we knew it was right. We had to pursue what God had put on our hearts, regardless.

We attended different churches on Sundays, so we could assess the spiritual climate of all denominations in the local area. Each couple made their own choice as to which church they visited, although most weeks Kevin and Andrea joined us. It was not an easy time and I certainly would not recommend being a spiritual gypsy, wandering from church to church, but for us at that time it was part of the preparation for what lay ahead. Once a week, all twelve of us would meet together in our home and pray, study the Bible and listen to what God had to say to us. Out of that came the idea to approach the governors of the school Adam attended, Blanford Mere Primary School, as to the possibility of hiring the school hall each Sunday. The building was known to all in the vicinity and was very easily accessible. After much deliberation, the governors agreed, but the start had to be delayed until the autumn. That was fine by us because it gave us several months to prepare.

Matthew was progressing really well; no broken arms or legs, no major hiccups! He loved attending playschool and going to swimming lessons with Adam on a Saturday morning. Life had resumed some sort of normality. Our fortnightly visits to the hospital were going well, with Matthew having only monthly general anaesthetics, but it was during one of these visits, in the early summer, that it happened again. We were sitting in the consulting room, waiting for the blood test results, when we were told that Mattie had had another CNS relapse.

'No! Not again!' I screamed. 'How can he? He's had no headaches or vomiting.'

'We're sorry, but he has had an asymptomatic relapse – a relapse with no symptoms. There are definitely leukaemic cells in his spinal fluid again. It's highly likely he will begin to show symptoms very soon,' we were told.

I cannot put into words what Paul and I felt. It was as though the bottom had dropped out of our world. Mattie's future, as far as medical knowledge was concerned, was very bleak. They had already inferred that his condition had become incurable, but now it had become a reality. The phases of remission, if any at all, would become shorter and the relapses more frequent and prolonged. We asked if there was any treatment available anywhere else in the world, but they informed us that there wasn't. The UK's treatment at that time was the most successful in the world. There was nowhere else on the planet we could take him. His tiny body could not tolerate any more intense treatment – it would kill him.

Paul and I looked at each other and knew, without saying a word, what we had to do. Together we explained our decision to the team of experts. They knew we were 'born-again Christians' and had been praying for Matthew's recovery; as indeed had many thousands of people around the world. We had placed our child in the hands of the medical experts and they had done a fantastic job at trying to eradicate this horrendous disease from our son's body, but they had failed. As far as Paul and I were concerned, there was only one course of action left: to withdraw him from the programme of treatment and ask God for a miracle. There was not one protest from the team. I think they knew that they had come to the end of the road with Mattie. We agreed to palliative treatment – treatment to relieve symptoms and discomfort – if necessary, but no more chemotherapy. They still wanted to monitor him every two weeks, to which we agreed. They warned us that by withdrawing him from treatment it would cause the leukaemia to spread far more rapidly. That seemed insignificant when they were only giving him three months to live anyway. It was highly unlikely he would even reach his fourth birthday. However, that was our decision and the medical team abided by it. We then had to go home and give the awful news to our family and friends; something, unfortunately, to which we had become accustomed.

I can remember going home that day and praying, 'Oh God, give me a normal four-year-old little boy, whose body is free of cancer and whose head is full of hair, and who can do all the things a four-year-old should do! Will you please do something that the medical teams can't – make the leukaemia go away?' I so wish now I had prayed for God to give me a little boy who would grow up to be an ordinary 70-year-old, bald grandfather.

Those next few days were surreal. Darkness seemed to surround us once again, yet there were a few flickers of light in that gloom; two in particular. Pam, my friend who lived close by, had been truly concerned about us as a family, always offering to help out in any way possible. When she heard the news of Matthew's second relapse, she was devastated. She could not understand how Paul and I coped; how we could even still attend church. She wanted to know how we were able to carry on living as we did. The only thing I could put it down to was the reality of our faith.

We were actually living out a passage from the Bible, Psalm 23:4: 'Even though I walk through the valley of the shadow of death, I will fear no evil, for you are with me; your rod and your staff, they comfort me.'

I went on to explain my journey to faith to her. She raised the obvious question of 'How can a loving God allow this to happen to children?' My honest answer was, 'I don't understand, but I know he does, because he went through a very similar situation himself.' The question of why it should happen to someone who believes in God was also troubling her. My answer to her was, 'Why not? We all share the same planet and breathe the same air. Christians haven't been sprinkled with magic stardust that gives them immunity to sickness and disease. Cancer, unfortunately, is part of life for many people, whether directly or indirectly. It attacks indiscriminately and in most cases unexpectedly.'

The only comfort I could give Pam was what I had received myself. I offered to pray for her and introduce her to Jesus, who had become my Prince of Peace. Pam accepted my offer and gave her life to Jesus that summer's day. The presence of the living God came into her lounge that afternoon and her life changed from that moment on. I couldn't take her to my church because I hadn't got one, but I soon hoped to remedy that situation. I spent time praying with her and encouraging her to read her new Bible.

During that same week, I had an almost identical conversation with another woman, Joan, Tessa's mum. Tessa was the little girl who had been diagnosed a few days after Matthew. Joan and I became very close friends, sharing joys and sorrows. Tessa had responded extremely well to the treatment – the only one out of the four in the original bay who had. Danielle, the other little girl, had received a bone marrow transplant a few months earlier. It had appeared to be successful, but the day she was due to go home she died.

Joan was extremely upset by the news of Mattie's second relapse. Of all our friends, she knew what this meant. She had watched how we had reacted to all the difficulties of Matthew's treatment and could not understand how Paul and I had coped without the help of medication or alcohol. Most of the parents were collecting regular prescriptions from their own GP in order to simply carry on living. Many had become dependent upon alcohol to relieve the pain of watching their child suffer. Paul and I needed neither. She wanted to know why, so I repeated my story of faith. Joan found Jesus as her Lord and Saviour and her Prince of Peace that day in her own lounge.

It took two weeks for the symptoms to manifest. The headaches began to occur and we knew we had to return to the hospital before the vomiting began. Mattie had another general anaesthetic, and another dose of methotrexate was injected into his spine to relieve the discomfort, but no other treatment was given. We returned two weeks later, on our ninth wedding anniversary, for a check-up and another dose of methotrexate; he had had no more symptoms, so his treatment was extended to a monthly basis. Matthew was not expected even to be alive by the September, but to everyone's amazement the lumbar puncture tests revealed a major reduction in the cancer cells. An injection was still given, however. The final shot of methotrexate was administered in October. We had been on this journey long enough to realise that cells could 'hide'. Just because they didn't show up didn't mean to say they weren't there. However, we chose not to put him through any more treatment if cells were not presenting themselves, and the medical team gave us no opposition. In our opinion, the quality of life was more important than the quantity, particularly when the latter was negligible.

Mattie had a great fourth birthday. He wanted a party at home that year and I was more than pleased about that, as McDonald's parties only held bad memories for me. We held it during the day, which, being midweek, meant that Adam was at school, and by the time he arrived home, most of the children had left. However, the party for family members continued for another few hours.

Mattie wanted just seven of his closest friends to come. As the birthday boy, he sat at the head of the table, holding court. He was more than capable of carrying out that role; he played it very often with both adults and children in attendance. The design of the cake was based on his toolkit, but the figurative icing on the cake was the weather: it was a glorious day, with temperatures way above normal for that time of year. After the children had feasted on party food, they spent the rest of the afternoon playing out in the garden and in the field; the farmer had harvested the crop just a few days previously, with an avid admirer looking on, hoping for a chance to ride in the tractor. That was a birthday worth remembering and I hoped there would be many more. Thank God I never knew what circumstances would surround the next one!

8

Indian Summer

The preparations for the launch of our new church had been made and the opening service was planned for the last Sunday in October. That weekend would certainly be teeming with activity. Paul was due to lead the Roadshow – a monthly interdenominational worship meeting, held in the local town hall with a thousand people in attendance – on the night before the opening, and Matthew had been invited to his friend Nicola's third birthday party on the same afternoon. Mattie didn't manage to go to many birthday parties, so he was very excited about going to Nicola's. He had been there for about half an hour when we had a phone call from Pam to say that Mattie wasn't very well. He had suddenly gone very pale and what she could only describe as 'spaced out'. He responded to questions, but something was not quite right.

Les, Pam's husband, carried him round the corner back to our house and returned to his daughter's party. Almost as soon as we laid him down on the settee, he began to convulse. In all the months of illness, he had never had one convulsion. There was no apparent reason for the fit – no temperature, no obvious onset of illness, nothing. It was about 5.00 p.m. and Paul, along with Kev, was due to leave for the final practice before the Roadshow that evening. Should we phone for an ambulance or rush Mattie over to the children's hospital? If we responded in either of those ways, Matthew would have to stay in hospital for a few days and the opening of the church would have to be delayed. Matthew was far more important to us than anything, but at that moment in time we really felt there was more to this situation than met the eye. We were convinced there was some unseen spiritual force trying to stop us doing God's will. It appeared as though Mattie was being used to prevent the weekend plans from going ahead.

Kev and Andrea were at our house within minutes of me phoning them – they had recently bought a house in the same street in order to be near the new church work. By the time they arrived, Paul was holding Matthew in his arms and praying for him. Gradually Mattie became much calmer, though he was still unconscious. Paul was so convinced that Mattie would be all right that he and Kev left for the Roadshow. I had total faith in my husband's convictions and encouraged him to go ahead with his plans. There would be time between the practice and the start of the meeting when he could phone home.

Andrea stayed with me and we continued to pray for Mattie. What thoughts must have been running through her head, I will never know. These experiences were not good for her – she was five-and-half months pregnant with her first child! By the time Paul phoned to see how he was, Mattie was not only conscious, but was eating his tea and ready to start playing with Adam again! Whether that convulsion was physical, spiritual or a mixture of both, we will never know, but he only ever had one other convulsion after that.

There were no after-effects the next morning. With great joy but immense apprehension, we walked into the school hall for the first time. Holding hands, our two boys led the way. We expected all twelve of us to turn up, but we were surprised to see a few new faces there; some we recognised, some we didn't. On that first Sunday, there were about 16 people in the morning service and 30 in the evening service. The children's club followed the morning service and to our delight more than 20 children came, many of whom were Adam and Matthew's friends. At a cost of £70 per day, we had signed a six-month contract to hire the school for two sessions every Sunday. Necessary equipment had already been purchased in advance of the launch, but since there were only two salaried people and four pensioners, this really was a 'faith' venture. There was no way we could afford that much money and no amount of budgeting would meet the costs, but we knew we were doing the right thing. We were hoping that the offering that Sunday would amount to several hundred pounds so that we could at least cover the first month's costs. To our amazement, the first day's offerings came to £3,000! The following week it was £1,600 and there was never a week after that when it was less than £100! Where it came from, I will never know. One of the first lessons we learned from those early days was that the Bible is as true today as it was when it was written. Philippians 4:19 says, 'And my God will meet all your needs according to his glorious riches in Christ Jesus.'

November brought us great joy. Adam's birthday that

year was free from trauma. The boys were getting excited about Christmas and Adam decided he wanted to write a letter to Father Christmas. He wrote asking for a Transformer and a Lego airport for himself and because Matthew could not yet write, he asked for some Fabuland Lego for his brother. Much to their delight, Father Christmas replied, stating he would do his best to bring them what they had asked for . . . he also asked for a mince pie to be left out for him!

A greater joy was ours when at the end of November Matthew's lumbar puncture stated that no leukaemic cells had been detected. He had gone into natural remission. We asked if we could be transferred to a three-monthly check-up and the doctors agreed. I think the medical world was totally bemused by what was happening.

We had a wonderful Christmas that year and Father Christmas did bring the boys what they asked for! The only problem Mattie had was a 24-hour throat infection, which occurred sometime between Christmas and New Year's Eve, but a course of oral antibiotics soon cleared it up.

Towards the end of February, Andrea gave birth to Christopher. During the last few months of her pregnancy, Mattie would sit on Andrea's lap, look down the front of her dungarees and ask, 'Where's the baby?' His confusion was still not fully resolved with Christopher's arrival. When he first held Christopher, he was absolutely amazed. He looked from Andrea's tummy to Christopher and back again, but didn't ask any further questions!

For the first time in nearly two and half years, we had three months free from hospital visits. When we took Matthew for a check-up in April 1986, the hospital could find nothing wrong with him. Since Mattie's diagnosis, we had been unable to leave the country. Because there was a marked improvement in him, we asked the doctor if it was possible to take him abroad on holiday. The answer was 'yes'! We left the hospital corridors, crossed the dual carriageway, went straight into the travel agent's and booked a holiday to Spain for the following month!

Matthew had never been on a plane before and was so excited about flying. He wanted the window seat and Adam willingly gave it to him. They were so thrilled when we taxied to the runway and their screams of delight matched the roar of the engines as we took off. However, as soon as the plane banked, Mattie turned to me and said, 'I think I'll get off now, Mummy!' His concerns were soon dismissed by Adam's ability to make him laugh and take his mind off his worries. We had a fantastic holiday in Mojacar. It was the first time since Mattie's diagnosis that we had felt like a normal family. I had a normal four-year-old, doing the things all normal four-year-olds do. God had answered my specific prayer.

Very strangely, there was a family at the same hotel whose son went to playschool with Matthew. We became quite friendly with them during that fortnight. Paul and I took it in turns to look after the boys. It was while I was having one of my 'time out' sessions that a woman came running up to me to say, 'Your son has just jumped in the pool.' I was not overly concerned, as Adam was a very good swimmer for his age. It took a few seconds for it to sink in that she was referring to Matthew, not Adam. Paul had been watching the boys playing in the paddling pool but then had turned around to talk to these new friends.

Matthew interrupted his dad to ask if he could go swimming in the big pool and Paul asked him to wait a few minutes. Not because of his illness, but because of his personality, Mattie had the ability to get his own way in a lot of instances. He knew he required armbands and adult supervision, so he interrupted again. Paul asked him, once again, to wait for a minute, but Matthew decided he had had enough of hanging around for his father, so with his baseball cap on, and minus armbands and adult supervision, he jumped into the pool – at the deep end! He went down, and then bobbed back up. It was at that point I screamed across the pool to Paul. By the time Paul reached him he was coming up for the third time, still with his cap on! Paul did what every parent probably would have done: hauled him out of the water, shouted at him and then hugged him. Paul questioned him as to why he had not waited and his simple reply was, 'Well, I wanted to go swimming but you didn't; so I went.' Mattie was not in the slightest bit traumatised by the affair, but we were.

Our next visit to the clinic was at the beginning of July. The report in his medical records states: '8th July 1986 – Matthew is remarkably well.' He had been off chemotherapy for over twelve months and all obvious signs of leukaemia had gone. This was the longest time throughout the whole of his life that he had had a full head of hair. The medical team were amazed at what had happened; a year ago his prognosis had been no longer than three months, particularly with the termination of treatment. To us, everything now looked hopeful, but the medical team would only rejoice in the present circumstances.

Matthew had a wonderful summer; he was well enough

to enjoy the freedom of playing outside with his friends. Adam led the way on his go-kart and Mattie followed on his red tractor, with his trailer attached, carrying his toolkit in case either vehicle broke down. Very often I watched them whiz round the corner to play with their Japanese friends, Yukiko and Tadasugu; Mark and James sometimes joined them. When they played on the green outside Pam's house, with Paul and David frequently joining them, she would very often bring them home. If no one was playing there, I took them down to the other green where Michelle, Samantha and Hannah lived; Sandra, one of the mums, brought them home. On the odd occasion, Mattie sneaked round the corner on his tractor to where Tash and her older sister Bec lived. He would sit on the opposite pavement and talk to them, knowing full well that he was not allowed to cross the road. More often than not they took pity on him and crossed the road to play with him. It was either Bec, or the girls' mum, Trish, who had the back-breaking job of pushing the tractor and Matthew back home up the hill, with Tash in tow. Very often the playtime would continue in our house or garden while the mums came in for a cup of tea.

It was looking very likely that Mattie would be well enough to join Adam at school at the beginning of the September term. Autumn is the season of beautiful rustic colours in Britain. For us, the last three autumnal seasons had been shaded with many dark and dismal hues, but it appeared that the forthcoming autumn was going to be different. Thankfully, we did not see the dark clouds gathering on the horizon.

▲ August 1982.
Matthew, aged 10 months, enjoying the attention at a wedding reception
with Paul and his grandparents.

▲ August 1983.
Adam and Matthew just before Matthew's diagnosis.

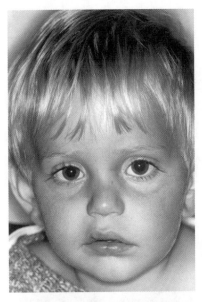

◀ September 1983.
Official hospital photograph
of Matthew on diagnosis of
leukaemia, age 22 months.

▲ July 1984.
Our wonderful boys, Matthew, aged 2½ yrs and Adam aged 5½ yrs.
Matthew's hair had regrown after radiotherapy.

▲ August 1984.
Matthew's determination to control the tractor outweighed
Adam's attempt at humour.

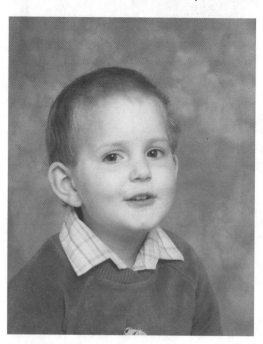

◀ July 1985.
Taken at
playschool. His
mischevious look
still obvious
despite the
ravages of
treatment.

▲ July 1986.
The last photograph of Matthew.

▲ November 1986.
A cheque was received from Matthew's swimming club after a sponsored swim in his memory.
Back row: Sandra Shakespeare (swimming coach), Gail, Paul.
Front row: Adam and Andrew (Matthew's best friend).

▲ December 1986.
Paul and Gail handing over a cheque for £4,500 to Dr Jillian Mann (now Prof. Jillian Mann, Emeritus Consultant Paediatric Oncologist) at Birmingham Children's Hospital in memory of Matthew.

9

Facing the Inevitable

Even though we had spent two weeks in Spain during May, we booked another week in St Ives, Cornwall, for the August bank holiday week. Every year since Matthew's diagnosis, we had spent our summer holidays there. The hotel we stayed in was very convenient; it was just a short walk from the end of the garden down to the beach and to the town. Because it was situated at the top of a rather steep hill, we used to hire a beach hut for the week. It was used to store our beach equipment and a change of beach clothes for the boys. On many occasions it proved to be a very good shelter from the English summer showers. Mattie would call it the 'hutch'; a rather apt name since it was made of wood and had a split barn door.

During the summer months, the hotel was very popular with families, so there were always friends for Adam and Matthew to play with. Even though my boys were four and seven years old, they somehow grabbed the attention of teenagers. I understood how Adam and Mattie could perhaps charm a few impressionable young girls, but it was a mystery to me how they could gather a group of modern, sporty teenage lads and entertain them for several hours. I have many wonderful memories of our boys either burying or being buried by them on Porthminster beach.

We had had so many good holidays down there and we convinced Paul's parents to come with us. I'm so glad they did. However, it was somewhat disappointing for several reasons. The weather that year was appalling; it rained every day, some days continuously. We hired a beach hut as usual, but it wasn't used much, except for sheltering in. Cramped conditions prevailed with four adults (Paul's dad was six foot four inches tall) and the boys on our laps. All we could do was drink tea and Ribena and watch the rain pour down.

On one really wet afternoon, we abandoned the beach hut and decamped to a café in town – it was even too wet to walk around the shops. While we were sat watching wet holiday-makers with umbrellas walk past, a rather macabre scene unfolded before our eyes: passers-by suddenly stood still, older men took off their caps and shop-keepers left their tills and stood in doorways; everything came to a halt. The reason for this interruption then came into view: a funeral cortege. It was not like the normal procession where the hearse leads the other cars. This one was very different; the top-hatted bearers were carrying the coffin on their shoulders through the cobbled streets of St Ives. From somewhere in the background came the haunting sounds of the traditional death march. The mourners were vast in number, all dressed in black. It was like a scene from the previous century. Adam and Matthew immediately asked what was going on. I simply replied, 'Someone has died and their friends are saying goodbye to them.'

Normally, they would have continued to ask further questions, but not that day. It was as though the spirit of silence that pervaded the drenched crowd outside had seeped into those who were sheltering from the storm. The mortality of mankind subdued everyone who watched the procession. Something very dark and foreboding entered my spirit that afternoon. Something I wanted to dismiss, but couldn't.

If there were any accidents going to happen, major or minor, then you could guarantee Matthew would be the casualty. Sure enough, one occurred on that holiday. Thankfully it was a very minor one, but Mattie had to experience it. We were sitting at the dining table ready to eat one evening, when Paul was pestered by a wasp. He knocked the wasp away with the back of his hand and it disappeared. The next moment we heard a terrific scream from Matthew. The wasp had somehow been catapulted down his tee-shirt and had proceeded to sting him! Paul felt absolutely awful – Mattie had received the sting that was meant for him.

The last day of the holiday was not good. Not only was the rain still pouring down, but Mattie was not well; he felt queasy and was sick several times. There was no point in stopping in Cornwall any longer, so we decided to go home. Within a couple of days Matthew had stopped being sick and seemed to pick up, but he remained somewhat subdued. I hoped it was due to him having concerns about leaving me and going to school, but that would have been totally out of character for Mattie. I couldn't shake off this foreboding that I had felt in St Ives; it was as though I had brought it home with me.

In an attempt to leave these feelings aside, we prepared

for a new school year. Mattie was so thrilled with his uniform. I had bought him a few new items, but most were what Adam had out-grown. Matthew was never bothered about wearing Adam's clothes – he felt as though he was emulating his big brother. If only those garments could have enveloped him with the same health and strength as Adam had!

Our boys were so excited on that first morning of term; Adam with the thought of playing the 'big brother' role, and Matthew at the prospect of starting 'big school'. I stood in the school playground along with the other mums and watched my little boy line up. I was so overwhelmed; there had been so many times over the past two years when I had thought I would never see that moment. All day I watched the hands on the clock slowly move round as I wondered what Mattie was doing and whether he was coping. I knew Adam would look after him at play-time and dinner-time, but how would he cope with PE?

I needn't have worried. His charms worked on a little girl, Sarah, who very kindly fastened the top button of his shirt. At dinner-time Adam took him under his wing and helped him to collect his lunch of chips and beans. They sat down and Adam introduced him to his friends. Mattie's response was totally out of character, and he declared to the whole table of lads, 'I love my big brother.'

At the end of the school day, most of the children came running across the playground, eager to tell their mums all about their first day. Mattie walked very slowly and it was Adam who gave me the details, not Matthew. As soon as we arrived home, Mattie lay down on the settee and watched TV. I expected him to be tired after his first day at school, but

I felt it was more than that, although I did not share my feelings with anyone, least of all Paul. I didn't want to alarm him unnecessarily.

The following day was Friday and I thought that Matthew could cope with another day at school and then he would have the weekend to recover and hopefully be a little more energetic by Monday. I decided to catch up on some housework that day. It was while I was doing the ironing that I received a phone call from the headmistress. Mrs Beswick knew all about Matthew's medical history and was obviously concerned. She told me that Matthew was not well and for the past hour he had been lying down on a settee in her office. I left immediately to collect him. As soon as he saw me at the door, he stretched out his arms towards me. My heart sank.

At home I sat with him on my lap and watched his favourite TV programmes. I was oblivious to what was happening on the screen – my mind was elsewhere. When Paul came home from work I told him what had happened. We both fell silent. There was no change in Matthew on the Saturday and his normal eagerness to participate in Sunday activities at church was gone. We knew we had to return to the hospital. I didn't sleep that night.

The next morning, as I was dressing Mattie, I noticed tiny purple spots over his arms, legs and buttocks. I had seen these on him once before – on diagnosis, three years ago. Oh God! I knew what was wrong with him. I didn't need any specialist to tell me. Without making a fuss, I showed them to Paul and he froze. Our eyes met; no words were needed.

I took Adam to school and informed the headmistress of what was happening. Paul rang the ward at the children's hospital and told them we would be arriving within the hour. We didn't give Matthew anything to eat or drink because it was highly likely he would have to have tests that involved him having a general anaesthetic.

Fortunately, Dr Mann was on the ward when we arrived and we were able to speak to her. She had grave suspicions that this was a relapse, but needed blood, bone marrow and lumbar puncture results for confirmation.

While Matthew was in the operating theatre, Paul and I waited in the parents' room, trying to find comfort in the warmth of a mug of tea. As I glanced at the coffee table, I noticed a small familiar booklet called *Daily Bread*, each day providing a Bible reading with a thought to follow. It had been read by another needy parent and left open on that day's page. It was only when I picked up the booklet that I realised the date was the 8th September – three years to the day since Mattie was first diagnosed with leukaemia! I looked at the Bible reading for that day and couldn't believe my eyes. It was Psalm 91. We had been in the very same room three years ago and read that exact psalm! When I had read it then, it had given me comfort and hope that Mattie would pull through. This time I had a different response. The thought that followed the reading was all about death. It went on to explain that death, for a Christian, was not the end but the beginning and that at the moment of death, a Christian would be face to face with their Friend and Saviour, Jesus. In heaven there would be no darkness, no pain, no more tears or sadness. A verse of a hymn, declaring God's faithfulness in all situations, followed the thought and there was a final prayer for anyone who was facing the prospect of death.

As I read that page, my mind flashed back to something Mattie had emphasised over the past three weeks; something that was both out of character and out of context. It was as though he needed me to understand something that was very special and very precious to him. His words flooded my mind at that moment: 'Mummy, Jesus is my special Friend. He's with me all the time. You leave me at night when you go to bed, but he doesn't. He stays with me. He never leaves me.'

This was it! The time had come. We didn't need any doctor to tell us the leukaemia was back. We didn't need any consultant to tell us that Mattie was going to die. We knew. God had used that little booklet to prepare us for the devastating news we were about to receive.

There were tears in Dr Mann's eyes when she spoke to us. She confirmed that Mattie had had a total body relapse; leukaemia was in his blood, his bone marrow and his spinal fluid. There was nothing else they could do apart from control the pain. They gave Matthew no more than three months to live. We wanted to take him home and care for him there; they agreed with anything we wanted. They would make the necessary arrangements with our GP, including any nursing support we may need. Dr Mann also suggested that she write to Matthew's school, informing them of his relapse and prognosis, thus lessening a little of the trauma for us.

Oh God! How could we tell our parents that we had lost the battle? They had been so strong for us, never once speaking about the possibility of losing Mattie. Oh God! How were we going to tell Adam that his brother was going to die very soon? Oh God! How could I carry on living without Mattie? I wanted to run away, but where was there to run to? My little 'Braveheart' needed his mum more than ever now. He had faced his illness with enormous courage, he had overcome setbacks with great fortitude, but he had now come to the end. I had to be strong to the bitter end; I could not let Mattie down now.

As we walked out of the hospital into the October sunshine, the darkness of death seemed to envelop Paul and me. Our grief could no longer be contained and we sobbed in each other's arms. We had already travelled a difficult path, but the worst was still to come.

10

The Last Lap

On the journey home, with guarded speech, we made our decision about what to tell the family. Thankfully, Mattie was too young to understand what was happening to him and an explanation was not required. We were not going to lie to Adam, but unless he asked a direct question, we would not tell him that Mattie was going to die. However, our parents had to be told the whole truth.

Paul drove home and stayed with Matthew while I went to our parents. As soon as my dad opened the door, he knew. He saw it in my eyes. He just held me tightly, but it couldn't make the pain go away. My mum appeared with her Zimmer frame, tears flowing down her cheeks; the silence in the hallway had spoken very loudly to her. Their words of comfort could not help me. Dad was 65 years old and Mum was two years his senior; they never expected to be in that position at their time of life. In 34 years of marriage, they had never experienced such anguish. I wanted to comfort them, to protect them, but I couldn't. I left them weeping in each other's arms.

The previous week Paul's mum had fallen down in the kitchen and broken her right kneecap. She was in plaster from her toes to her thigh and was hobbling around the house on crutches. At 72 years old, it was too much of a struggle to climb the stairs, so she slept on a single bed in the lounge. Not surprisingly it was Paul's dad who came to the door. As he opened it, I couldn't say anything; I just shook my head and cried – the lump in my throat had become engorged. He just stood there for several seconds in disbelief. Then the tears started flowing and the heavy sobs began. Such a gigantic frame of a man became crippled with grief. He staggered back into the lounge, fell into a chair and held his head in his hands and sobbed. Mattie had held a special place in my father-in-law's heart that no one else was ever able to fill. I tried to console him, but he was in a state of shock. Paul's mum lay on her bed weeping, calling Mattie's name over and over again. When I left, she was struggling to get out of bed to try and comfort her husband of 35 years. Both sets of parents would have willingly taken Mattie's place if they could.

As I drove home, I resolved to be as strong as possible for my two boys. I was going to have to pack a lifetime of motherhood into a few short weeks for Mattie. I was determined to make them the most meaningful, the most loving and the most treasured of all. They had to be – it was my last chance. The possibility of Adam becoming emotionally scarred, even with what he had already been through, was very high; this last lap was definitely going to have a profound effect upon him – for the rest of his life. There was very little I could do to cushion him from it.

The next two or three days were surreal. I gave Mattie

regular doses of prescribed diamorphine, which helped relieve his discomfort and thus gave him the ability to play with those toys he could sit down with. Adam went to school as normal. Nevertheless, our son was dying and there was nothing anyone could do about it. Over the last three years we had watched other children die from cancer and it was one of the worst things we had ever seen. The final journey can be so drawn out. The agony for both patient and parent is terrible. It was with these thoughts in our minds that we changed the way we prayed for Mattie. Instead of asking God to heal him, we prayed that he would 'take him home to heaven' – quickly. We begged God not to let Mattie suffer any longer and for it all to be over very soon. I did not want to have to carry memories of a slow death with me for the rest of my life. 'No more, God! Please take him quickly!' I pleaded.

I never asked God why this had to happen, but I did ask the medical world how it had happened. No one could give me a categorical answer. We were told that Matthew was genetically predisposed to cancer, but that alone did not cause it to present. It was the unknown factor – the missing link – that kicked it off. My mind travelled back over the last three years; memories of events brought queries that flooded my thoughts. Did the pylon in the field behind our first home have an effect, or the electricity substation in the drive next door to that house? That was the home in which Mattie was conceived! Did the measles virus trigger the onset? Did all the X-rays encourage the relapses? What about the Chernobyl disaster earlier that year? Surely that must have had an effect! The radioactive cloud from the nuclear explosion extended for thousands of miles, covering large parts of Asia and Europe, stretching westwards over the UK and lasting for 15 days. I was looking for an answer; something, not someone, to blame. But I couldn't find what I was looking for.

For the first time in three years, Paul and I found ourselves talking about what we needed to arrange for Matthew's funeral. We had never even spoken of the possibility of his death, and now we were talking as though it had already happened!

By this stage, both sets of parents had retired and were available to help, although they were somewhat restricted with the disabilities of our two mums. My parents and Paul's dad didn't miss a day coming to see Mattie. On the Thursday, three days into the 'death sentence', my dad took Mattie out in the car. He couldn't push both my mum in her wheelchair and Mattie in his pushchair, so Mum encouraged my dad to spend some time alone with his grandson, while she stayed at home with me.

The following day, Paul's dad came and took Mattie out alone. On many occasions he had taken his beloved grandson to Himley Country Park and they had spent hours picking up sticks, collecting conkers and kicking up autumn leaves. Now it was only one of them picking up and collecting, while the other carried the autumn treasures on his lap in his pushchair, too weak to do anything else. While they were out creating precious memories that would last my father-in-law his lifetime, the headmistress, Mrs Beswick, and Matthew's teacher came to see him. I was glad they came when they did because it gave me chance to speak openly to them. They patiently waited for Mattie to come home. The shock at the decline in his condition, in just a week, was written across their faces. Both of them put on a brave face, but struggled to hold back the tears. I watched as they walked to the car, pulling out handkerchiefs and wiping their eyes.

Mattie loved what we called 'bits and bobs', preferring them to his large expensive toys. On the Saturday morning, he asked his dad for some new ones – hinting at a trip to the toy shop. Paul immediately took him to the nearest one, drove through the pedestrian precinct to get to it and stopped right outside the shop! He carried Mattie in his arms, because he no longer had the energy to walk.

Mattie was getting worse. We knew that Paul's mum couldn't come down to see him, so that afternoon we made one last journey to take Mattie to see her. She had not seen him for nearly a week and the shock was too much for her; she had to turn away and weep. Of all the grandparents, she was the one who had rocked Adam and Matthew to sleep when they were babies, disregarding my request to put them down to sleep. Once she had control over her emotions, we placed Mattie in her arms one final time. No words passed between them, just a loving gaze connecting soul to soul. I was oblivious to the smell of death that was surrounding Mattie. She wasn't, but she didn't say anything. She knew that would be the last time she would ever see her youngest grandson alive.

We were still running the church and many more folk had joined us over the year. It was very rare for us to miss a Sunday, but I knew it was out of the question for me to go. My place was by my son's side. Through all the trauma of the week, Paul was still able to get the framework of a sermon together. Just how he did it, I don't know. I think it must have helped to take his mind off the situation. Barbara, one of my friends who had recently become a Christian and who had started attending our church, came to stay with me on the Sunday morning while Paul and Adam went to church. Mattie was starting to lose control of his bodily functions, so there was rather a lot of washing to do, including several lots of bedding. She insisted I sit with Mattie while she did all the work. She left when Paul returned, leaving behind a chicken cooking in the oven, but taking all the ironing with her. There was only Adam who was hungry. Paul managed to eat a little; Mattie tried but began to heave and not a solid thing passed between my lips.

Pam, my friend who had offered so much practical help, came to stay with me Sunday evening while Paul and Adam went back to church. This was the larger service of the two, where there were regularly 30 or more in attendance. Other than the original members, all the others were new Christians. No one really expected Paul to turn up, but they had wanted to meet together anyway to pray for us. Pam and I decided to watch *Songs of Praise* on TV, searching for comfort in our faith. I couldn't believe it when one of the hymns sung was the one I had read in the parents' room of the hospital just a few days earlier. It was as though God was speaking directly to me, confirming that he would be with us through this 'valley of death'. He would never leave us.

Within minutes of the hymn finishing, Mattie had a convulsion. Pam rang Paul at the school where church was held and he dashed home, followed by his dad and my parents. He rang the ward at the children's hospital and asked for an emergency home visit because we knew that if we took Mattie to hospital at that stage, we would never bring him home again. The hospital knew our situation and complied immediately. It seemed like an age waiting for the doctor. We felt helpless as we watched our darling son convulsing. It was getting too much for Pam, but she didn't want to leave, so she went and stood outside to wait for the doctor. Paul's dad left for home before the doctor arrived, desperate to inform Paul's mum of recent developments.

The doctor lost his way. It was nearly two hours after Paul made the phone call that the doctor arrived, apologising profusely for his delay. Pam had waited outside for most of that time. By that stage, the convulsions had eased, although they had not stopped entirely. The doctor warned us that there would probably be side-effects, as this appeared to be more of a stroke than a convulsion. He said that it was highly likely that Mattie had lost the use of one side of his body. It turned out that he was correct in his diagnosis. I could no longer cuddle him because he was in too much pain; he had become very sickly and we had difficulty giving him his medication. 'Oh Mattie! What are we doing to you?' I silently screamed as the doctor inserted a suppository – a necessity for pain relief. There was only one higher level of pain-killer left – an injection of morphine – and he was reluctant to administer that until the very end. It was midnight before the doctor left, closely followed by Pam and my parents.

I had put Adam to bed soon after he returned from church, encouraging him to gently kiss Mattie. Amazingly, he slept through the entire trauma. Paul and I decided that Mattie should sleep with me in our bed and Paul should sleep in Mattie's bed. I spent most of the night stroking his face – the only part of him that seemed to be free of pain.

He appeared to be sleeping from time to time, but I wasn't sure whether he was slipping in and out of consciousness. Paul didn't sleep very well; several times throughout the night he helped me to change the bedclothes.

The following day Paul took Adam to school; we wanted to keep as much normality as possible for his sake. When he returned we brought Mattie downstairs and laid him gently on the settee, padding him with pillows as much as possible. My parents arrived mid-morning, closely followed by Paul's dad. By lunch-time Mattie was hardly speaking, only replying to my questions with one-word answers, and struggling even to do that. I could eat nothing at all, but Paul made a sandwich for himself and my mum and dad. Paul's dad went home and then returned for an hour or two later in the afternoon.

In all the years of Mattie's illness, I had never seen him so poorly; there seemed to be an invisible cloak enveloping him and I was unable to protect him from it. I had been giving him the diamorphine suppositories, as directed by the doctor. No mother should have to do that to her son. The only way I could do it was to see it as my last act of love for my precious little boy. It was the only way I could relieve his pain. I had to do it.

Mattie's breathing became somewhat irregular and laboured. My dad had been at the bedside of many family members during their last few hours and he knew what to look out for. At his suggestion we phoned our GP and asked for a home visit. The hospital had informed him of recent developments and asked if he would be willing to be on call should we require a visit. He was very apprehensive, but felt it was an honour to serve us to the end.

It was around 10.30 p.m. when he arrived. Our own doctor had not seen Mattie for quite a time, and he was shocked at our son's appearance. He thought that the suppositories were no longer having any effect, so he moved onto the final phase of pain relief: an injection of morphine. He told us it would probably allow him to be more peaceful. Not long after the doctor left, Mattie closed his eyes. Little did I realise that I would only have one more final glimpse of them and then they would be closed for ever.

Once Adam was in bed he had the ability to sleep through anything and I was so thankful for that. Before Mum and Dad went home, Dad helped Paul carry our king-size mattress downstairs. There was no way we were spending the night apart. Mattie was too ill to be disturbed, so we had to come to him. As Mum and Dad left they were insistent that we ring them if there was any change in Mattie's condition – whatever the time!

We sat on the mattress for hours listening to Mattie's rattling breaths, watching his tiny chest heave up and down. At one stage we turned off the light and attempted to get some sleep, but it was hopeless. No blackness of night was going to rob us of the final hours with our son. We sat in silence. No words could express how we felt. There were no words left to say.

It was during those hours that Paul and I understood a little more of what Jesus meant when he was being crucified on the cross at Calvary and cried out, 'My God, my God, why have you forsaken me?' We couldn't feel the presence of our God. We felt deserted, abandoned, frightened and devastated. This was no nightmare – this was reality. There would be no daylight relief from this horror.

11

The Anguish of Dawn

I gazed through the window and watched the dawn. Outside it was growing lighter, but in my heart I felt no sunrise. I knew deep within me what this day would hold. It would be a day that no parent should ever have to live through.

The vast majority of other people would have a normal day. Tuesday 16th September 1986 was a working day for everyone else. Fathers would be getting ready to leave for work and mothers would be getting up to prepare breakfasts and packed lunches for their children. Within a few hours the streets would be busy with cars being driven on the school run and with mothers manoeuvring pushchairs, hastening their energetic children to school. Many would take the time to chat at the school gate, while others would rush off to work or back home to do the chores they were unable to do with children around them. Oh, how I wished this could be the type of day that lay ahead of me; but it wasn't. Oh God, how could I face this day? How was I going to walk the path that lay ahead of me? I wanted to do all I could for my beloved son, but at the same time I wanted to run away. How could I be a good mother and still think these things? I realised that the moment I turned around and left the outside world behind, my darkest day would begin. This would be the last day of my role as mother to my darling Mattie and I was going to give him everything I could. Nothing would stop me fulfilling this. And so it was with these thoughts running through my head that I finally drew myself away from the 'normal' outside world and turned to face my 'Calvary Road'.

As I turned my face away from the world outside, my heart began to break at the scene that appeared before me. I had never seen Paul like this before. Here was the man I had loved and who had been part of my life for 17 years; the man I had married ten years previously and with whom I had shared everything; the man who had given me all he could; the man who had given me Matthew. As he sat on the mattress, he gazed upon his son with tear-stained eyes. Even through the mist of tears, I could see the love emanating from his eyes. The love he had for his son was so evident. To the outside world he appeared a broken man, but to me he had become Herculean. My love for him deepened that day.

What thoughts were racing through his mind I can only imagine. Was he wishing for more moments of kicking a football around the garden with Mattie? Was it the realisation that he would never stand on the sidelines, supporting him in his school football team? He would never cheer him as he scored a goal. Never watch him pick up prizes at school. Never have to love him through the rebellious teenage years. Never have to load up the car and take him off to university. Never have the opportunity to sit in a university hall and be bursting with pride watching his son's graduation ceremony. Never be asked fatherly advice about the things in life that really matter. Never see the boy become a man. Never see him marry, let alone perform the ceremony. And never watch him become a father himself.

Not only was he losing a son, but grandchildren as well. Paul has always found it very difficult to express his feelings and thoughts and to put them into words. His strong silence was his way of handling the situation, his way of dealing with his emotions, and I had to respect this.

My eyes then turned to the object of his loving eyes. How could this be happening to our family? The beautiful baby boy whom I had given birth to almost five years previously was lying there fighting for every breath and I could do nothing except watch the battle. The time between each gasp seemed an eternity, and when he eventually drew one, it took every fibre of his being to gain sufficient strength to do so. His frail body shook with the effort of trying to draw in vital oxygen. When he managed it, the noise that heaved from his lungs was horrendous. He was almost drowning in the fluid that was accumulating in his lungs. I had heard of the so-called 'death rattle' before, but nothing could have prepared me for this. It was the most remorseless, blood-curdling sound my ears had ever heard and yet I was not terrified. I had loved Mattie from the moment he was born; I would love him through this, his final journey and on into eternity. Nothing, no sound, no sight, no smell, absolutely nothing would ever quench that love I had for him. I wanted to breathe for him. I wanted to take his place. I wanted to make everything better. I couldn't.

The effects of the previous day's stroke upon his little face were no longer evident, since he was not using any facial muscles. This, however, was of little consolation, because the hours of darkness had brought a different mask to my beautiful boy's face. Blood was now oozing from his ears and nose. I was watching my four-year-old son have a brain haemorrhage and I could do nothing to help him. No plaster, no bandage, no hug from Mummy could staunch this flow. That little blond head, which had borne the most obvious effects of all his years of chemotherapy, was now leaking with his precious life-blood. All I could do was gently dab the precious droplets. Oh, how I wanted to go and wash that blood clean of cancer and put it back into his body, cancer free. But I couldn't.

The smell of death had been around for some time, but it was now much stronger. His body was ceasing to function; his cells were dying one by one. The intimate aroma of the bond between mother and child slowly faded as the cloak of death was silently and invisibly wreathed around my son. That sickly, sweet-smelling stench had permeated everything: his body, his hair, his clothes, the bedding he was lying on. We smelt of it; the room smelt, the house smelt. The strange thing was, the longer this nightmare lasted, the more acclimatised to this deadly perfume we became. This was now part of Matthew and in order to get close to him I had to inhale this mysterious odour.

The colour of his face had changed: it had become grey. His lips were no longer the little rosebuds they once were. The texture of his skin had become clammy. Oh, how I wanted to hold my son closely and tightly, and never let him go, but I knew I couldn't. Even though he was in a coma, the memory of a few hours ago, of the pain he was in even when I just touched him, was still uppermost in my mind. I was frightened to touch him, let alone hold him.

The night had reached out its tentacles and drawn him deeper into a coma. The doctor had warned us hours ago that this would happen. At least when he was in a coma he was showing no obvious signs of discomfort. This coma was welcome in the sense that it was relieving the previous situation, but at the same time it was taking my son further away from me.

The hours drifted slowly by, but time was of little importance to us now. So it was a shock when the doorbell rang. True to his promise, the doctor arrived well before his surgery was due to start. He confirmed that Matthew was slipping deeper into a coma and that it would be a good idea to phone all close family members who wanted to be there and whom we wanted to be with us. This was the doctor's way of saying that it would soon be over. I heard myself asking how long it would be, not really wanting to know the answer, and I remember his faltering reply: 'Gail, it's like his birth was: we know it's imminent, but we can't give you an exact time.'

He was the sole doctor at the practice, but nevertheless he promised to return after morning surgery. I knew we could have called in any of the doctors from Birmingham Children's Hospital, but they didn't know us like our own GP did. His father, who had owned the practice before him, had welcomed me into the world. As wonderful as these other doctors had been, and as hard as they had tried to rid Mattie of this horrendous disease, we no longer wanted strangers around us. If our own doctor hadn't been able to handle the situation, then I would have called them in, but he was handling it, albeit very emotionally.

I did not know that my parents had sat up all night, dozing in armchairs, waiting for the sound of the phone; they had wanted to be prepared for our call. Within half an hour of receiving the phone call, they were walking through our front door, knowing that when they returned home it would be in a state of mourning. As my parents entered the lounge, my mum's eyes went to her grandson, but my dad's eyes rested on me. I had become his little girl again, and I sank into his loving arms. This time, he couldn't sort it out for his precious daughter; he couldn't take the pain away. We wept in each other's arms. Mum hobbled round the room to her grandson and very gently, very lovingly, stroked his head. Once my father had comforted me, he transferred his attention to Mattie. With his weathered hands, he caressed Matthew's face; his tears mingling with Matthew's blood.

Matthew was the apple of my father-in-law's eye. The difficulty of communicating the severity of the circumstances, and knowing the depth of his love for his younger grandson, made it very difficult for Paul to make the phone call to his dad; only stunted sentences were uttered. Paul's mum was unable to come; I don't think she would have handled the situation very well. When his dad arrived, their silence spoke deeper than any words. Grief and sorrow needed no voice.

Adam soon awoke. How we wanted to spare him from the pain that this day would hold! How we wanted this day not to be embedded in his mind and heart for the rest of his life! But today was destined to be a part of his life story, and I could not prevent it. The presence of his grandparents was enough to set alarm bells ringing in Adam's mind. I encouraged him to kiss Mattie before he left for school, but I said nothing else to warn him of what the day might hold. However, Adam was very astute and I suspect he knew exactly what could happen. To create a diversion in his thinking, my dad took him to school, something he had never done before. The school was aware of the situation and was prepared for him to be collected at any time of the day, should it be necessary. I wanted to give Adam the chance of one final day of normality – if you could call this normality.

12

Day of Departure

Normality was something that was happening in the outside world, but not for me. I watched from the window as my friend Margaret left to take her driving test. It must have been difficult for her, knowing what was going on in our house. How I longed to be where she was right then – leaving her son for just a few hours, while I was going to leave mine for the rest of my life. She arrived back with confused emotions: delighted at passing her test, but distraught for her friends.

Soon afterwards, Andrea arrived with Christopher. Was it just a few weeks ago that Mattie had sat in her lounge, with Christopher in his arms, and said that he would teach him how to play football? That was never going to happen. That was the first of four visits Andrea made that day. Soon after she left, her husband Kev arrived. He could not stay at work when his best friends might need him. He remained for most of the day.

Not long after he arrived, I saw a lone figure struggling up the road, and it took a second before recognition dawned. It was my elderly aunt, who had travelled on two buses to make one final journey to see Mattie. Breathless and exhausted, she staggered through the door. Renee was not a blood relative, but had been my mum's best friend for nearly 50 years. I had always referred to her as 'Aunty Renee'. When she eventually took her eyes off Mattie, she went to her friend of many decades; they just clung to each other and wept. Kev drove Aunty Renee home; it relieved the intensity of emotion for him, which he was finding difficult to handle.

Throughout that time Mattie's condition remained unchanged. We no longer consciously thought each breath would be his last. Although I wanted this torture to be over, at the same time I did not want to let him go. Not yet. Just a little longer.

For the past few days, Paul had put an updated message on the answerphone each day. I had become deaf to its almost constant ringing and was no longer interested in who was trying to contact us. However, one phone call did arouse my concern. Paul had taken a call from a stranger who attended a church in London that had been praying for Matthew. He wanted to come and pray for him, along with two other friends; a journey of over a hundred miles, taking several hours. I really could not believe that Paul had given them directions to our house. What was going through Paul's mind at the time I couldn't begin to imagine. Thousands of people had been praying, and indeed were still praying for Mattie. Perhaps Paul was grasping at one final straw of hope, or perhaps he just felt lenient towards their compassion for us.

To say that I was disgruntled about this was an understatement, but it was not the right time to enter into a verbal debate. Paul was not in a condition to think logically, and as a result he never took a contact number for them, so there was nothing I could do about the distinct possibility of strangers turning up on our doorstep at the very moment we wanted isolation from the rest of the world. The last thing I wanted was a well-intentioned but highly unwelcome intervention by a stranger. I had to dismiss this from my mind and focus on my Mattie. Anger was the last emotion I wanted rising in my spirit at that time.

I refused all nourishment that was offered to me. The thought of food just made me feel sick, but I did manage sips of water. Strange thoughts of personal deprivation ran through my mind. How could I feed my body at a time like this? How could I give it nourishment while my son's body was dying? My body was 32 years old; his body hadn't even lasted five years. I wanted to put him back in my womb where he had been for nine months. He would have been safe and secure within my body. It would have been my body that protected him; my body that fed him; my body that took all the stress and strain. In there, darkness would have held security and warmth. In there, he would have had no need of lungs – no need of vital oxygen. In there, no struggle for life would have taken place; life would have been ahead of him, not behind him. It should have been my body lying there, not his. If his body was unable to take food, then neither would mine!

Even though all those who dearly loved me surrounded me, I felt so alone. The desolation sapped my strength. The darkness in my soul became fathomless. I felt as if I were drowning in it. There was no more fight left in me. I had spent the last three years in combat alongside Matthew against this abhorrent disease. We were now into the final battle and I knew we had no weapons left. My son had been remarkably brave and had won so many victories, but it was finally drawing to a close. This precious child of ours had fought gallantly and with great dignity. I had to face these last few hours in the same way. I had to obtain strength from outside of myself, and there was only One who could give me what I needed. But where was he when I needed him the most? Why could I not feel his presence in this dark period? The next hour would bring with it a totally unexpected dilemma.

It was around 1.00 p.m. when the doctor returned. He greeted, or rather acknowledged, the familiar faces of my parents, for he was at a loss for words. We later found out that Mattie was the first child in his practice to be diagnosed with leukaemia; this was new territory for him.

He informed us that Matthew had slipped deeper into a coma and that he would never come out of it again. We would never make conscious contact with him again. Dear God, he was slipping away from me; he was falling and I couldn't hold on to him! I would never look into the depths of those beautiful brown eyes again. Never again would I watch with envy those eyelashes we called 'road-sweepers'. We had not heard his wonderful, chirpy little voice for a day or two; the only sounds he had made over the last 48 hours were cries and moans of agony, followed by the awful gasping resonance caused by his lungs making their final attempts to get oxygen. This was torturous – watching him disappear, one function after another ceasing. I wanted the end to come quickly now.

With these thoughts racing round my head, the doctor

confirmed our suspicions that Mattie was having a brain haemorrhage, but he also indicated that the ordeal was by no means over. If Mattie was still alive by midnight, the situation would become even more distressing. Not only would his precious blood continue seeping out of his head, but also his vital organs would collapse and he would experience major internal bleeding, which would distend his already ravaged body. Pneumonia would set in and the sound from his lungs would be even more harrowing. At this final stage, his little heart would be unable to take any more and he would suffer a fatal heart attack.

I knew when I left the normal world outside my window at dawn that what lay ahead of us would be like no other day, but I had never, on my darkest days, imagined the end would be so horrendous. I just wanted to erase that day from our lives. It wasn't happening to us! I hoped I would wake up in a moment and it would all be over. But no, this was for real. My heart was breaking and my head was swimming with the probability of those final conditions arising. My body was in the same room as everyone else, our ears were hearing the same words, but I was shot through; I could take no more.

We were thankful for the doctor's honesty and compassion. The shock of hearing all that caused confusion in my mind when he went on to make a suggestion. What he actually said, and what I thought he suggested, were probably two different things, but it brought me back to reality with a jolt. Did I hear him correctly? Was he offering to boost Mattie's dose of painkillers for the right reasons, or was I looking beyond the words and imagining more than that? Was this the way out of our dilemma? No! I must not allow myself to think such things! Paul's response brought me back to the moment: 'We can't make a decision so vital in a matter of seconds or even minutes. We shall have to think about it and talk it through.'

'Well, you haven't got very long left. I'll be back after the evening surgery, at about 7.00 p.m. You can let me know your decision then,' were the doctor's parting words.

Matthew was in such a deep coma that we felt he did not require any more painkillers. To administer morphine at this point, in our opinion, would not have been for analgesic purposes, but alternative reasons, although it certainly would have been justified by the fact that he hadn't been given any medication for well over 14 hours. The doctor would definitely have administered it on medical grounds, but our permission would have been given based upon something else. No one would have been any wiser, except us. What a decision for any parent to have to make! We certainly didn't want Mattie to suffer any more; neither did we want to go through any more heartache or put our ageing parents through any more distress. To make a similar choice for oneself is one thing, but to have to make it for another human being is a different matter entirely. In reality, we felt that if we agreed to this, the main reason would have been to hasten the death of the son we had given life to. What if God wanted to miraculously intervene at the very last minute? If we agreed to this dosage, then we would be playing God. No, I couldn't live the rest of my life knowing that I had made the final choice, not God. Paul came to the same conclusion. No matter how hard the last hours were going to be, we would see it through God's way. Mattie came into this world naturally; he would leave naturally. His birth was in legitimate circumstances; his death would be likewise. We had made our decision: no more morphine! It was the finish of years of first-rate yet futile treatment. No more medical intervention; nothing. It really was the end of the road.

It was at that point that we made our final drastic plea to God, not to heal Matthew but to take him. We were desperate to feel our Lord's presence, for up to that moment we had felt nothing since dusk the previous day. Where was the 'peace that passes all understanding'? 'Oh God! If ever we needed you, we need you now. Just come into this trauma and sort it out,' I cried.

It was 2.00 p.m. exactly when the atmosphere in our lounge changed. It happened in a split second and everyone felt it simultaneously. It was as though a presence had entered the house. It certainly wasn't frightening or imposing; more peaceful and reassuring. It had the aura of a Person, but I couldn't see him or touch him. None of my natural senses could confirm his presence, but he was there. I had experienced closeness to my Lord before, but never to this degree. I could hardly breathe with the density of the holy atmosphere.

And I wasn't alone in this experience. We looked from one to the other in amazement; the change in the atmosphere was unbelievable. It was several moments before we realised another change had taken place: Matthew's breathing had become placid. The deep, laboured guttural tones of his breathing pattern had been transformed into silent, shallow pants. All of us were now more at peace. My head tried to persuade my heart that Mattie was on the road to recovery, but my heart knew different.

It was during those silent moments that an amazing analogy came into my mind. I saw life as a race; Mattie, by that stage, had reached the 'home straight'. He hadn't run countless laps; his race hadn't been long distance, but it had involved many hurdles. Now the finishing line was in sight. All his loved ones were in the stands, cheering him on as he made his final steps – a few more strides were all he had to make. But it wouldn't be us who would be on the track to embrace and congratulate Mattie when he reached the tape; that would be Someone else's job. His Friend and 'Coach', Jesus, was waiting for him on the finishing line. This gave a little clarity to otherwise confusing circumstances.

My role was definitely coming to an end. How I wanted to freeze-frame that moment, even turn the clock back! But time was not in my hands. It was actually slipping through my fingers like sand. Only a few precious grains were left and I was holding on to these very tightly.

Many friends, who had been so supportive of us, desperately wanted Mattie to win his battle and would be devastated with the inevitable outcome. I wanted to give some of these a last chance to see him, particularly those who were neighbours. So it was with a heavy heart that I stepped out into the normal world.

I didn't have to think about Adam; he was safely ensconced in school and a friend would bring him back. Margaret wasn't at home; she had gone back to pick up Andrew from school – something I would never do again for Mattie. So I continued down the road, and as I did my mind began to recall memories – good memories of the hours I had spent walking along those pavements. The first time was with Matthew safely in my womb; my steps had been very laboured, but not as heavy as they were now. So many hours had been spent manoeuvring his pushchair up and down those paths, Mattie shrieking with laughter. Many of those moments were on the playschool run with Adam by his side, always making him chuckle. I had taken great delight in the pleasure they had found in each other's company. I would never walk those streets with him again. Never collect him from playmates' homes. Never stand in the window and watch him play outside. Many hearts would be broken by the close of the day. Everyone who had known him, adults and children alike, dearly loved Mattie. My heart and my arms would be empty when I next came that way. That was a heavy load to bear and I didn't want to carry it, but there was no other way.

Both Mavis and Sandra wanted to see Mattie one last time, but Mavis had to find someone to look after James. Both of them had spent many hours with Mattie as our children played together. Our estate had a very strong community spirit, which was probably the reason why there were so many young families.

From Sandra's house I walked up the road to where my friend Barbara lived. When she saw me, she realised the gravity of the situation. With tears in her eyes, she refused my offer; she couldn't cope with the emotion she was feeling. The whole state of affairs was too close to home for her to handle. Paul, her eldest son, was Adam's best friend – the one he sat by in class, the one with whom he walked up and down to school, the one who had been his first friend in playschool. David, her youngest son, was born just four months before Mattie, and they had played and fought together. She would continue to give me all the practical help she could, but it was too emotional for her to see Mattie again. We just hugged each other on her doorstep, our tears mingled. No more words were said.

Pam was the last one to call on. As I approached the house I recalled the times I had spent here with Mattie; the hours he had played with Nicola, the joy they had shared as they had entered her Barbie doll world. Not every playtime had been harmonious, particularly when they both wanted the same Barbie doll or Ken's car. Mattie had loved to get his own way, and most times he had succeeded. Heavy medication had received the blame, but I suspect it was more his feisty personality. I'm sure God had given him that characteristic so that he was able to cope with his illness. I recalled the day, just over a year before, when I had introduced Pam to my best Friend, Jesus, in her lounge. Her life changed for the better that day; the future impact would be far greater than I could ever have imagined. That day, a year ago, I had brought her good news; now I was the bearer of sorrowful tidings. She was grateful for a final opportunity to see Mattie, but she had to get someone to look after Nicola. Apart from Kev and Andrea, there was no one else with whom I wanted to share Mattie's final moments.

I made my way back home, knowing that the next time I left it would be as a grieving mother. The mind can play very strange tricks on a person in a time of anguish. In one sense, I didn't want to return; I thought that perhaps if I didn't enter my world again, it would remain frozen in time. I would have done anything to arrest the situation: maybe, if I never went home and had no contact with the family, then Mattie might live. I would have been prepared to pay that price, if it could have guaranteed life to my son. But that wouldn't have resolved the plight my family was in. We were destined to travel this road of suffering; it was unavoidable. As I walked the last few steps, I prayed that I would have the ability to see these last few hours through with grace; that I would be able to savour every moment left with Mattie. I wanted to be able to recall these hours years later. I wanted them to remain as very special, precious memories. I had to trust that someday, somewhere, someone would benefit from this traumatic experience.

As I walked through the door, the atmosphere was so thick, so full of the presence of Jesus. Paul's dad had returned, as had Kev and Andrea. Everyone was silent. Sandra was the first of my friends to arrive. As she walked through the door, she drew a sharp breath. She wasn't a Christian, but she could sense something different in the room. Death was on the doorstep, but it wasn't only death that she sensed. She literally couldn't speak because of the presence she felt. With tears streaming down her face, she stroked Matthew's cheeks and gave him one final kiss. She then turned to look out of the window; with her back towards us, her shoulders heaved with muted sobs. Not wanting to put us through any more grief, she hugged me and left in silence.

Mavis was the next to arrive. She had a similar reaction to Sandra; she knew there was something strange about the atmosphere, but not being a Christian she couldn't fully recognise what it was. She knelt beside Mattie and held his hand; there was no response. With tear-soaked lips, she kissed his hand and said her goodbyes to him. She then left my world behind and stepped into the normal one outside.

These two dear friends didn't have the faith that I had. They didn't know my Saviour, so they had to carry their grief alone. In one sense, they were worse off than I was. My Jesus was carrying me. I could feel his loving arms around me; I no longer felt alone. I knew that he wouldn't leave me now.

Pam was the last visitor to see Mattie alive. This lady with whom I had struck up a friendship on the way to taking our sons to playschool was to become a woman who would support me through many dark days. Pam, whose compassion and kindness, whose mercy and sympathy were so evident during those last days, entered our home one final time. It wasn't on a mission of mercy, but a final chance to say goodbye to a little boy who had affected her life so incredibly. She was so grateful for this opportunity we gave her. So many people will want to greet Mattie in heaven and thank him for the way he affected their lives; I know she will be one of them. She left our home that afternoon having experienced the presence of God in the direst of circumstances. Confusion and grief flooded her heart as she walked to the end of the drive. So much so that she couldn't remember which direction to take in order to return to the safety of her own home. She walked to the right, stopped; turned left, stopped; then eventually went home in the right direction, crying all the way.

Kev and Andrea decided to take Christopher home. They felt the time had come when only family should be with Mattie. They said goodbye to our parents, held us and just cried. Kev's hard exterior had melted and the soft compassionate heart shone through. They knew they would never see Mattie alive again; the little boy with whom they had spent so much time, on whom they had learned to change a nappy. They kissed him goodbye and left.

Paul's dad was next to leave. A giant of a man, he got down on bended knee to say his last goodbyes to his grandson. With tears flowing from beneath his spectacles, he kissed his beloved Mattie: this little boy who had given him so much joy in his old age. True to form, he arose, kissed me and shook his son's hand. He was not usually tactile, even with family members, but in no way did this reflect the love that father and son shared; they were very close.

It was around this time that another change in the atmosphere took place. We had felt the presence of Jesus for some hours, but up to this point nothing obvious had altered in Mattie's condition other than his breathing becoming less laboured. Now there was a subtle change. His body was still functioning, but it was as though my son was no longer confined to his dying body; his spirit was free. It felt as though he had once again gained the freedom to play in the safety of his own home, but this time with his faithful Friend Jesus. No matter where I went in the house, I felt their presence, together. I watched my son's body to see if his little chest was still rising. It was. Not much, but it certainly was. I had no logical explanation for what I was experiencing, but it was very real. So much so that I felt able to go upstairs and have a shower and wash my hair.

As I stood in the warmth of the cascade of water, my mind tried to rationalise what I was doing. I was showering while my son was lying on the sofa dying! He might die while I was doing so and I would not have another chance to be with him. I knew exactly what I was doing, and why. I wanted to remove the stench of death. I wanted to look my best for Mattie one final time. I wanted him to smell the sweet perfume of his mum one last time. My tears mingled with the freshness of the flow of the water; they became one and the same. Finally, I dressed myself – in bright colours – and made my way downstairs.

13

Final Moments

My parents seemed to have aged in the 20 minutes it had taken me to shower. They had been at the deathbed of many folk, but never did they imagine they would be at this one. This was not nature's way. It should have been the other way round. Dad felt useless; he wanted to do something practical to help, so with great relief he collected Adam from school.

When Adam came through the door, he immediately went to his brother. To him, Mattie seemed a little better because his lungs were no longer making the rasping sounds that he had heard earlier on in the day.

Adam had received very little attention over these last three years, but never once had he been resentful. My memories of him over those three years are non-existent. How can a mother's memory of her first-born child be eradicated from her mind? I have no answer; but they appear to have gone for ever. How I wished the same could have happened for him of the memories of that day. But I was not the one in control of his mind or emotions.

Paul took him upstairs to have a game of snooker – anything

to take his mind off the situation. We were still trying to keep everything as normal as possible for Adam; he was still only seven years old. After a few games, he wanted to come downstairs to sit by his brother and hold his hand. It was as though he knew the time of Mattie's departure was drawing close. Children have a more simple understanding of certain things that unfortunately is lost in adulthood. All of us were broken-hearted as we watched Adam very gently hold Mattie's hand for the very last time. They would never speak to each other again; never see each other again. They would never again play together, never again fight together. The two best friends would not grow up together; they would not do things together as teenagers or grown men. They would not be together to support each other. Adam was going to have to see it through by himself.

We had arranged with Pam that when we felt time was coming to an end, we would take Adam round to play with her son, Russell. We didn't know how we were going to react in the final moments and we didn't want to traumatise Adam any more than was necessary. 'Kiss Mattie once more and say goodbye,' I managed to utter. We didn't need to tell Adam that he wouldn't see his brother alive again; he knew. With a final kiss, and parting words of 'I love you, Mattie', Adam left the house.

Both sets of parents had been a source of strength to both Paul and me; we had felt their support all through the difficult years. Never once did they refuse when we asked for their help. So there was no way we were going to dismiss my parents in these final moments. They chose to stay.

It was just after 5.30 p.m. that the final stage of Mattie's pilgrimage began. Paul's parents were back at home and it must have been so difficult for them not knowing exactly what was happening. Thank God, we had made it to this stage without any interruptions from well-intentioned strangers! Even the telephone had remained silent for the last half an hour. For some unknown reason, we decided to gather around Mattie. The presence of Jesus was still very tangible, regardless of the circumstances; peace reigned in our home. I sat on the settee with Mattie; Paul knelt by his side; Mum and Dad sat on chairs next to us, looking over Mattie like guardian angels.

The only sounds to break the silence were the sobs and snuffles coming from the four of us, and the hushed, shallow breathing of Mattie, whose lungs were almost deflated. The smell of death had grown stronger throughout the day, but it had almost reached its zenith now. We had become so intoxicated with it that we were oblivious to its presence. His body was almost drained of fluids and his precious lifeblood was being swallowed up by death. His pallor was such that his lips were indistinguishable from the rest of his beautiful face. The texture of his skin had changed from clammy to cold. My motherly instincts told me to get a blanket and make him warm. But it was pointless. He was beyond any need of warmth.

And then it happened. He opened his eyes. He was conscious and recognised us. Paul's initial reaction was, 'He's had no painkillers for over 18 hours, and he'll be in pain.' But he wasn't. There were no signs of discomfort at all. My reaction was, 'God's done it! He's healed Mattie! He's back!'

But it was my dad who saw the truth of the situation. With a shout, he brought me back to reality: 'Gail, hold him! He's going!' I was so frightened to touch him, but I knew this was my very last chance. And so, for one final time, I took him in my arms and held him. I knew that these next few moments would have to last me a lifetime. Paul held his hand and caressed him. My parents stroked his head. He was conscious through all of this and I believe he knew exactly what was happening. In the last seconds of his life, he looked first of all at my parents. He then looked at his daddy, the man who had been his guardian and his hero. And then his eyes turned to me. He was beyond speech, but he spoke with his eyes. It was as though he were saying, 'Mummy, it's all right. I'm happy. It's all gone. I love you and I always will. I'm going now, but I'll be waiting for you. Bye.'

Then he quickly turned his head to the corner of the room. It was as though Someone had called his name; Someone whom he knew very well; Someone who had never left him in the night watches. We saw no one, but Mattie did! A smile of recognition crossed his face and he left with his Friend. Mattie died in my arms.

Immediately, the presence we had felt so strongly for the last few hours disappeared, taking with him the soul of my son. I was left with his body lying limp in my arms. I stood up with him and a piercing sound emanated from somewhere deep within me and filled the room. It was as though someone had reached into my body and torn out my insides. This was a physical pain like nothing I had ever experienced before. The muscles of my lungs ceased to function; I had stopped breathing, but I was still holding on to my son. Paul took Mattie from me and held him very lovingly. It was a few moments before he realised the state I was in. He quickly handed his son to my dad and came to my assistance. He told me to breathe, but I just shook my head. I didn't want to breathe any more. He shouted at me to breathe, but the response was the same. He was becoming desperate at this point and began to shake me. I eventually drew a breath, but had to really concentrate to take consecutive ones.

I watched as both my parents and my husband tenderly held Matthew one last time and said their goodbyes to him. What a pitiful sight it was! Paul then had to make the phone call to his parents.

My dad suggested that he and Paul lay Mattie's body out; he felt that it shouldn't be a stranger who did this final thing for him. Dad knew that within an hour, stiffness would set in and it would be very difficult to arrange the body. They had both bathed Mattie from time to time and they wanted to do it once more. Dad had 'laid out' many old people in the past, but never a child. He wasn't afraid, however. Why should he be? Mattie was his grandson.

Paul brought Mattie's mattress downstairs and laid him on it. They very gently and tenderly washed and dressed him. Dad knew what he was doing. He wanted to make Mattie look as good in death as he had done in the good years of his short life. In death, the skin becomes taught, and features can look unpleasant. Dad didn't want this for his grandson, so he asked for a tea towel, which he compassionately wrapped around Mattie's chin and tied it on the top of his head; this was to keep his mouth closed. He then took two coins from his pocket and placed them on Mattie's closed eyelids. Finally, Dad asked for two large books and another tea towel. He supported Mattie's feet with the books and used the tea towel to secure them in place so that his feet would remain side by side. We decided to place his two favourite teddy bears in his arms: the one that Adam had given him when he was born and Mattie's favourite.

During this preparation session, my mum tried to comfort me. She was not only feeling the loss of her grandson, but watching the pain of her daughter; a pain that she couldn't ease. Because of her disability, she couldn't get as close to me as she wanted. I was motionless and in a state of shock. She came over to where I was sitting and bent over her Zimmer frame. She kissed and caressed me as best she could. It was quite a time before my mum realised that I had not spoken since Mattie had died. She called Paul back into the room and told him. All I could do was shake my head and weep. There was nothing more to say, so why bother? I really did not want to go on living; all I wanted was to be with my Mattie.

I was brought back to my senses when Paul said he was going to collect Adam. Adam! I had another son. I had done everything I could for Mattie, but he no longer needed me and Adam did. Over the three years of Mattie's illness, Adam had never really had my full attention. Well, he was going to get it now. I had to be complete for Adam. I would have a few minutes to get myself ready for consoling my son – my only son, Adam.

14

Goodnight and God Bless

When Paul approached Pam's house, Adam was outside with his friends, riding his bike. As soon as he saw his dad, he knew from Paul's face that Matthew had died. Pam watched through her window, willing Paul not to arrive with the dreaded news. But he did. Paul did not confirm Adam's worst fears until they were alone. As I gazed through my window, waiting for them to return, I saw such a heart-rending sight: Paul had his arm around Adam and the almost silent sobs could be seen emanating from both father and son as they pushed Adam's bike back home. The tears were streaming down Paul's face; what agony he must have gone through, telling his son that his brother had just died.

Adam walked through the door and ran into my arms. I just held his throbbing body – a body that had warmth; a body that held a heart that beat and lungs that inflated; a body that was racked with grief, but a body that was alive. After a few moments of comfort, he asked where Mattie was. I never thought for one minute that he would ask to see him, but he did.

Oh Lord, what a decision to make! These last days of trauma and intense grief would remain in his memory for the rest of his life. Would we be adding to that trauma, or would we be helping the situation if we allowed him to see Mattie's body? It wasn't as though we could take our time discussing the pros and cons. We had to be decisive. Adam had been with Mattie all the way through this awful illness and had seen him in a far worse state than he was in now. So our decision was 'yes'.

Dad went into the room first, to remove all the things he had used to prepare Mattie's body. This final act of love that he had performed for his grandson meant that apart from his ashen complexion and the stillness of his body, Mattie looked as though he was asleep. We held Adam's hand as we took him into what had been their playroom. He stood motionless, tears cascading down his cheeks and soaking his tee-shirt. There was no fear in his face, only intense grief. Right then, I would have given anything to be able to turn back the clock almost five years, to the moment he first held Mattie and introduced himself as his big brother, best friend and protector. Here he stood now, looking at his beloved brother for the last time. All Adam's hopes and dreams of a life together had died with his brother. His best friend, his comrade, his confidant, the one who one day may have been his best man, and the one who would have been an uncle to his children was gone.

Between sobs, we asked Adam, 'Do you want to say anything to Mattie? Do you want to touch him? Do you want to give him one last kiss? Do you want to be alone with him? You will never have another opportunity, Adam. This is your last chance.'

His answer amazed us: 'No, Mum. That's not Mattie. My brother has gone. This is only his shell. Like the shell left behind when an egg has been eaten.'

Where can a child of seven years get such profound insight? It certainly wasn't from us. This was the first taste of death our family had experienced. It was as though Someone was beginning to take away the sting of death for him already. What he saw that evening did not in any way terrify him, but consoled him. He saw that death was not the end. He felt his brother had gone somewhere else. He believed without a shadow of a doubt that Mattie had gone to heaven. Adam knew he had gone to be with Jesus. He said his final earthly goodbye to his precious brother Mattie, knowing he would see him again one day, in heaven. He had gone to be with the One whom Adam had heard him frequently talk of. The One he seemed to know personally.

Paul's father arrived soon afterwards. No words were exchanged between father and son, only a deeply emotional embrace. He went to say his final goodbyes to the grandson who had borne his illness so courageously. But no privacy could be found; the sound of his weeping filled the whole house.

The doctor was the next to arrive. He came out of the room with tears in his eyes. In a quivering voice, he offered us his most sincere condolences and handed us Mattie's death certificate. Cause of death: acute lymphoblastic leukaemia and cerebral haemorrhage. With a heavy heart, he left our home and our lives. We were sorry not to see him any longer, as he was almost part of the family, but within a few weeks we had changed our GP to one at a local practice, which was nearer to home.

Adam wanted to tell his friends himself. Russell's reaction was deep silence. Paul's was free-flowing tears. Adam needed to be with his two special friends; he needed some sort of normality after a very difficult day.

I needed to get out of the house, but as I left, the strangers arrived from London – the ones who had made the phone call earlier in the day. Paul handled the situation very well. He told them that they were too late; Mattie had been dead for about an hour. They left in tears; strangers who never even knew him!

I had walked across the road many times either to take or to collect Mattie from his best friend's house – that would never happen again. Margaret and John had gone to a parents' evening and Andrew was being looked after by his grandma. Thankfully, he was too young to understand the inferences I made to Gwen. It was not right for him to hear the sorrowful news from me or his grandma. He would need his mother's arms to console him. Nevertheless, he knew there was something wrong.

I couldn't face seeing anyone else, but neither could I return home. So I just walked the streets in a zombie-like state. I was so confused with the thoughts that raced round my head and the mixed emotions they brought. I eventually found myself walking back home. As I opened the door, the sweet stench of death greeted me. What a difference to the fresh air I had just breathed in!

Not long afterwards, Kev and Andrea arrived with Christopher. Reddened eyes and tear-stained cheeks were evidence of their sorrow. I silently took Kev by the hand, opened the door to the playroom and took him in to say goodbye to Mattie. What I didn't realise in my grief was that he had presumed the undertaker had already been and taken the body away. He never expected to see Mattie. This was the first corpse he had ever seen and I hadn't given him warning! He disguised the shock amazingly well. Gently he kissed Mattie goodbye. Not a word was said by anyone. I repeated the same procedure with Andrea, in total silence. There was nothing more to say.

Other friends arrived that night to offer their condolences. Some saw Mattie, others wished to remember him in life rather than death. My mum and dad were the last to leave. They had stayed the full course with us. They both went in to say their goodbyes to the grandson they had loved so much. My poor mum could not get down to kiss him, which seemed to heighten her grief. My dad had the consolation that he had done everything he could for Mattie – in life and in death.

Then we were alone: three of us now, not four. We had decided not to phone an undertaker that evening. For the last three years we had lived with other well-meaning people dictating to us. We wanted to be together for a few more hours. We wanted one last night with Mattie. After Adam had gone to bed without very much fuss, Paul and I went into Mattie once more. We still couldn't believe he had gone, even though the evidence was right before our eyes. We knew it was just his shell, but still a very precious one.

He had been part of me for nine months; I had given birth to him almost five years ago. How could it all be over so soon? Every night of his life we had prayed with him and this night would be no different. So with great love and affection but with heavy hearts, we gave thanks to God for allowing us the privilege of ever having Mattie. We asked for help and strength to get through the years that lay ahead of us. We didn't need to pray for Mattie any more; we knew where he had gone and who he was with. He was safe for eternity. He was home. We kissed him and completed the prayers with our familiar but final phrase of 'goodnight and God bless'.

We went to bed and held each other very closely. Eventually we fell asleep and slept soundly. How could that be possible with our child's dead body a few feet below us? We didn't have any medication from the doctor, even though it was offered to us. We didn't drink any alcohol. There can only be one answer: the peace that passes all understanding was with us – the peace of God.

Adam wanted to go to school the next day, so I took him in, but an hour late. Returning home, we phoned the undertaker and then called my friends to ask if they wanted to see Mattie one last time.

The undertakers arrived and after their condolences they asked us if we wanted a few more minutes alone with Mattie before they took him away. Paul and I had decided that we didn't want to go and see him in the chapel of rest, and certainly not in a coffin, so we went in to see our son for the last time. Paul knelt down beside him and with quivering lips, salty with tears, kissed his adored youngest son.

For my final moments, I lay down beside him, as I had done so many times before, and covered his sweet face with kisses that were moistened with tears streaming down my face. I told him that just as I had loved him in life, so I would love him in death and on through eternity. I promised him his life would not be in vain and that while I had breath his story would be told. I told him that he had been born for a reason far greater than the four years he had lived, and that one day that reason would be obvious to all who ever knew him. Then I gently wiped the evidence of my intense grief from his cold, waxened cheeks, got up and walked out of the room.

They didn't have a child's portable coffin, so they had to use an adult one. When the undertakers carried Mattie out of our home, they were crying. They had seen hundreds of bodies – death was part of their life – but this was different for them. I sobbed uncontrollably as the hearse took my son away. It was all over! What I didn't realise until a few days later was that at exactly the same time as the hearse drew up outside our house, another friend had turned up to visit Mattie, not knowing that he had died. What a shock for Dave. He just sat in his car a few yards up the street and wept. He couldn't face us.

We made the arrangements for the funeral and took instructions from the undertaker regarding all the legal procedures that had to be carried out. The next few days were surreal. The condolence cards and flowers came pouring in and messages were left on the answerphone. Visitors came and went, thankfully occupying quite a chunk of our time.

The funeral was booked for the following Monday, the 22nd September 1986. Paul had asked someone to cover his responsibilities at church for the Sunday following Mattie's death, but we still felt as though we wanted to go to church. We sought strength to help us through the next 24 hours. We needed consolation and comfort, and we knew where they were to be found. The folk at church were like an extended family to us. When we were hurting, they were hurting. They did everything they could to ease our pain. It may have been just a school building, but it housed the presence of God as much as any cathedral could.

It was only immediate family who gathered at our house to follow the funeral procession. This was the first funeral Adam had attended and I had briefed him on what the procedure would be. We had requested family flowers only, with donations for the Birmingham Children's Hospital leukaemia ward. As a family, we had bought two floral tributes: a small cross for the coffin and a replica of his red and yellow tractor which Mattie so loved riding. I had tried to prepare myself for the sight of a small coffin, but it still came as a shock to see it, knowing that my precious son's body lay entombed inside it. Thankfully Adam's attention at this point was focused on the cars and the fact that he was going to ride in one of them.

Because we used Blanford Mere School for holding our church services, we had to use another church for the funeral. We chose the church where we first went together, Eve Lane Pentecostal Church in Upper Gornal. It could easily seat 500 people and we knew there would be at least that number attending. We had chosen four good male friends to be the bearers, two of whom were Kev and Andre. Their grief-stricken expressions when we arrived more than replaced words of consolation. How I took those first few steps into the church I don't know. However, I was absolutely determined that I was going to walk down the aisle unassisted, with my head held high, proud to have been the mum of such a brave little boy. This was going to be a service of thanksgiving for his life, not a wailing ceremony.

I was taken aback by the numbers in the church; it was full to capacity, folk standing at the back and around the sides. Paul and I held Adam's hands to walk down the aisle; my parents followed, with my mother on her Zimmer frame. Next came Paul's parents, his father pushing his mother in a wheelchair with her broken, plastered leg outstretched. Finally, there were two aunts, one of whom walked with two sticks, and an uncle who was also a cripple. What a pathetic sight we must have looked! In the normal course of events, it should have been one of the older members of my family at the front of the procession, not Mattie.

So many people from various parts of our lives were there and friends from every stage of our lives, from childhood to present day; even some of our school friends from the Sir Gilbert Claughton were there. How well we were supported on that day. All the songs we had chosen were positive, not sombre. I held up quite well until the final song, 'Great is thy faithfulness'. This was the hymn we had seen in the daily reading booklet in the hospital just a few weeks before and also the one on *Songs of Praise* a few days later, the words of which had somehow warned us of Mattie's impending death, but had also offered us consolation, strength to get through this trauma and a promise of a future, which at the moment seemed very bleak. At that point I just wept. Adam looked up at me and tears welled up in his eyes. The three of us held each other very tightly. By the time I had to walk back through the church I had composed myself, unlike the majority of mourners who were there.

We only spent five minutes in the chapel at the crematorium. I took my last glimpse of Mattie's coffin as the curtains were drawn, and I knew this journey was finally over. Within a day or two my son's body would be ashes, blowing in the wind. To us, that was a far better option than the alternative. All of my energies now had to be centred upon Adam, who had been so brave and patient.

We returned to the wake at Eve Lane Church to thank our family and friends for the support they had given us, not only on that day but over the past three years. We had decided to have a part of the room dedicated to Mattie's memory, with photographs of his life, both in an album and on display. It was not morbid, but a celebration of a precious life. People were most grateful for the opportunity to see some of the cherished moments we had captured on camera. Very strangely, Paul and I found ourselves comforting others. How could that have been possible? We felt as though we were being enveloped by unseen arms and strengthened by an invisible force. I believe we were feeling the effects of hundreds of people's prayers for us. There could be no other logical explanation for our reactions.

When the last of our friends and relatives had left, we went home. All the frenzied activities of the previous weeks were in direct contrast to the emptiness we felt as we walked through the door. How different our lives would be from this point on. I really didn't know whether I could face tomorrow, let alone the rest of my life, without Mattie. My darling Mattie. It really was a final 'goodnight and God bless'.

15

Life after Matthew

Ithank God that I had Adam. He was the reason I got out
of bed the morning after Mattie's funeral. He was the
one who insisted on returning to normality; he wanted
to go back to school. That was one of the most difficult
school trips I've ever had to make. As I held Adam's hand,
the emptiness of my other hand was magnified. The reality
of Mattie's death began to dawn upon me. In a way, all the
funeral arrangements had distracted me from the grievous
loss we were suffering. By involving myself in these frenzied
necessities, I had occupied both my body and my mind in
activities still connected with Mattie, but now there was
nothing left to do for my younger son. Mattie was no longer
here; he no longer needed me. But Adam did.

Paul had gone back to work, so I returned to an empty
house. Even though Mattie had died there, it still felt like
home to me. It was where I last played with him, last heard
his voice and last held him in my arms. As I walked into his
bedroom, the emptiness consumed me. I slipped under his
duvet and tried to find comfort in the place where he had
found it. But it was not to be found. As my head lay on his

pillow, I was aroused by a familiar fragrance, one that only exists between mother and child. I could still smell Mattie's presence in his pillow. Something unique to Mattie was still around! I jumped out of the bed and opened drawers, frantically trying to find his aroma in other items of his clothing. I then realised that my friends had washed all of our laundry and had thus removed the last traces of his aroma. But then I remembered his dressing gown – the one he had died in. I had not included it in the laundry. I flung open the wardrobe door and there it was! As I held it to my face, the wonderful fragrance of Mattie filled my nostrils once again. I closed my eyes and embraced that dressing gown as though it still contained my beloved son. I got back into his bed with it still in my arms and wept and wept. How long I lay in his bed, I don't know, but the pillow was sodden with my tears.

I don't remember much of the first week after Matthew's funeral, except for one incident that had a profoundly positive effect upon me. Paul was still involved with the Roadshow and the September event was due to be held the Saturday after Mattie's funeral. Paul didn't feel ready to lead a thousand-strong celebration meeting, but we did want to go to it. I can understand how people can 'shake a fist' at God in times of grief, but to me God was not a Judge who had just handed out a death sentence, but my heavenly Father who longed to comfort me. All I wanted to do at that time was run into his arms and allow him to ease my pain, because no one else could, not even Paul, who was very compassionate towards me. I needed to be in God's presence as much as possible. And there was another reason why I wanted to get close to my Lord: I believed that was where Mattie was.

During the service, a local minister was invited on stage to pray for us, but it was no ordinary prayer that he prayed. He asked the audience to close their eyes and picture us. Then he asked everyone to pray about what they saw in their 'mind's eye'. As I closed my eyes, I saw a wonderful picture. It was of a photographic studio, where our family portrait was being taken. Paul and I were standing with Adam just in front of us and Paul's hand was on his shoulder. Mattie was in my arms, resting on my hip. Behind Paul and myself, with his hands on our shoulders, was Jesus. It was as though, in some strange way, I was transported into that scene and was actually living it out, but yet still watching it from afar. I categorically remember feeling Mattie getting heavier and heavier, and I was struggling to carry his weight. Then I saw myself turn around and hand Mattie to Jesus, turn back to face the camera, and place my hand on Adam's other shoulder. No one moved out of the picture frame; it was still our family, but Jesus was carrying Mattie, not me. The responsibility and the care of Mattie had been transferred to Jesus. That scene had such a profound effect on me and indeed, as the months and years unfolded, proved to be very prophetic. It is as clear to me today as the evening I first saw it. God knew exactly what I needed to carry me through the grieving process and to live my life post-Mattie.

Friends and family were very good to me during those first few weeks. They occupied a lot of my time, but I knew that I needed to adjust to the new life that had been imposed upon me. We received hundreds of sympathy cards and letters from around the world, some from people we never knew but who had been following our story.

Many of them contained verses from the Bible that helped somewhat. However, there was one particular verse that appeared time and time again and seemed to have a lasting impression upon us – John 12:24: 'Unless a grain of wheat falls to the ground and dies, it remains only a single seed. But if it dies, it produces many seeds.'

As I read this verse, it brought back memories of the hours we had spent with Mattie in our back garden, watching the farmer both plant and harvest his crops. Matthew could not understand how a single grain of wheat could produce an ear of corn; the two were so very different. In a simplified manner, I explained to him that there was more in that single seed than could be contained in its shell. So in order for it to reach its full potential, it had to shed its husk. However, it wasn't as simple as stripping away the outer layers and immediately finding an ear of corn. It had to be planted in the soil, alone in the darkness. Nature would take its course and time would do its job. Eventually, we saw the green shoots burst forth. As the sun rose in the summer skies, we watched the shoots slowly grow into full ears of corn, turning from green to yellow as they ripened. As we walked along the edge of the field, Mattie held out his arms at shoulder height, skimming the ears of corn with the palm of his hand, fascinated at the miracle of nature he had watched unfold. Because of his height, he couldn't see what I could, so I picked him up to view the wonderful vista before us – a whole field full of wheat, swaying in the gentle summer breeze. I plucked an ear of corn for him to examine up close. He was amazed at what was in his hand – a product of one tiny single seed. I never realised at the time how prophetic that all was.

There were incidents over those early weeks and months that were rather painful. There were people who crossed the street rather than speak to us. I realised they didn't know what to say, but I felt that even saying 'hello' would have been far better than ignoring us completely. However, there were things said to us that I would have preferred not to have been said. Things like, 'I know what you're going through.' 'No you don't; you're not me!' I wanted to scream back at them. Comments like, 'Oh, never mind; you're young enough to have another baby' really hurt us. The inference received, although not necessarily meant, was that Mattie could always be replaced by someone else. That was impossible. He was not to be equated with a car or appliance that had broken and needed to be replaced!

Several events also helped our grieving process. We were so thankful for all the help the Birmingham Children's Hospital gave us. The way they had fought so hard for Mattie's survival was more than commendable. We wanted to show our gratitude in a way that would be most helpful to them – fund-raising. In a matter of a few weeks we raised over £4,500. Donations in lieu of funeral flowers were accepted. Adam and Andrew took part in a sponsored swim at the club where Mattie had also been a member. Adam raised nearly £200 himself and Andrew, who beforehand could only swim one width, swam 20 non-stop in memory of his best friend!

I was aware of the fact that if I didn't remove Mattie's toys and clothes from our home very soon, I would never be able to do it. That was one of the most difficult things I had to do after Mattie died. Paul and I selected a few precious items that held special memories, and Adam and our parents did the same. (Even to this day we still have his dressing gown and his beloved red tractor with a broken trailer, and Adam has his tool bench.) The remainder of his possessions became items in a garage sale that Margaret held at her house. Without exception, all of my friends turned up at the sale with two purposes in mind: to raise money for the children's hospital and to have a memento of a very special little boy's life. I couldn't bring myself to attend; I was elsewhere that day. The remaining items were collected by a children's second-hand distribution company, which also made a contribution to the fund.

For the past three years I had been virtually confined to our house. I was distressed over the reason for the confinement but I found solace in my home. In the days following Mattie's death, that changed dramatically. Emptiness replaced the solace and I no longer enjoyed the comfort of the house I called home. I had to plan my days. Every day had to have a purpose. That was the only way I could physically function. I remember one incident, just a week or so after the funeral. I had gone into Wolverhampton to do some shopping. Unlike most women, I don't enjoy shopping, but I used the excuse to occupy my time. I was due to pick Adam up from school and I was running late. As I drove along the quiet dual carriageway (no doubt breaking the official speed limit), a thought crossed my mind: 'If I don't turn the steering wheel, if I just keep the car in a straight line, then without hurting anyone else I can be with Mattie in a matter of seconds.' The following second brought the response, 'But how will Adam cope without you?' I knew in that split second what I had to do – turn the steering wheel. My love for Adam surpassed my grief for

Mattie. I could not voluntarily put Adam, Paul or our parents through more grief than they had already experienced. I was consumed by grief, but I was not selfish enough to inflict even more pain upon those I dearly loved. Adam wondered why I flung my arms around him when he walked through the school gates!

I was dreading the 10th October – what would have been Matthew's fifth birthday – and wanted to stop time. It was bizarre. I received floral gifts instead of Mattie receiving toys. The need to buy something for him that day was overwhelming. I bought a dozen red roses, but when I walked out of the florist's, they seemed totally inappropriate for a five-year-old boy. So I went into the toy shop and bought a small red tractor. I returned home, put the flowers in my best crystal vase and placed it by a framed photograph of Mattie. As I stood the small red tractor in front of the vase, memories came flooding back of his birthday the previous year. The reality of it all began to dawn upon me. I would never celebrate another birthday with my son. I would never see him waken to his teenage years. Never have the joint eighteenth and twenty-first birthday party with Adam that we had dreamed of on the day Mattie was born. No more birthday cards. No more presents. No more Mattie. It truly was all over. How would I live through all the birthdays that he would have had? The 10th October from now on would never be the same again. God would have to help me through every one of them.

During Matthew's illness, we had had to avoid contact with any contagious diseases, particularly chickenpox, as it could have had fatal consequences for him. However, one morning, a few weeks before his eighth birthday, Adam woke to find himself covered in red spots – he had caught chickenpox. What perfect timing! Within days of the last spot disappearing, his features changed, resembling those of a hamster – he had caught mumps! It was as though both of these childhood diseases had been held at bay until Matthew was no longer around and could not suffer any more.

November held many challenges. Apart from Adam's birthday, we had to face another 'first' without Matthew. In the early part of that summer I had entered a competition to win a holiday. It had been run by one of the national newspapers, with questions on Wimbledon. Both Paul and I are not only tennis fans but members of both a local tennis club and the LTA (Lawn Tennis Association), so it was very applicable to us. I had answered the questions and Paul had written the accompanying slogan. In July, I had received a phone call, and to our surprise we had won first prize – a November departure for two weeks in a luxury villa on Portugal's Algarve coast, all expenses paid, including a daily maid and daily coaching sessions at the David Lloyd tennis centre. Originally, the prize had been only for Paul and myself, but when the editors of the newspaper found out about Matthew, they had wanted to pay for both of our boys to accompany us. They had requested permission to write an article featuring us winning the prize, which would have been published on our return. We had agreed to this request and had been interviewed and photographed at home. We had been so excited at the time, but the holiday had lost its appeal after Mattie had died. A few weeks after Mattie had gone I contacted the editor of the newspaper and told him that because of the loss of

Matthew, we no longer felt able to accept first prize. He rejected our refusal and insisted we leave the final decision until a few weeks before departure date. As the weeks rolled by and the reality of the loss of Mattie really sank in, we changed our minds concerning the two-week break on the Algarve. We had to learn to live again without him, in every area of our lives, both at home and abroad. No way would we have arranged a holiday so close to Matthew's death, but it was as though Someone else had arranged it for us, with no expense spared!

At that time, children did not have their own passports, so both Adam's and Matthew's details were written in mine. When we checked in at Heathrow Airport, we were not ready for one of the questions that was asked of us: 'Is Matthew not travelling with you today?' We were so taken aback that we just said, 'No.' I walked away from that check-in desk with tears rolling down my cheeks. 'Why on earth am I doing this?' I asked myself.

The villa was absolutely fantastic, but we could not really appreciate it. It was massive – in fact too large. Its size emphasised the void left by Mattie. Up to that point we had been surrounded by friends and family. Those two weeks gave us an opportunity to face life together as a family of three. As difficult as it was, it was absolutely necessary in order for us to begin again.

As I sat on the beach and watched children at play, my heart began to break. I remembered the summer holidays spent on Porthminster Beach in St Ives, Cornwall. I remembered peals of laughter coming from my boys as they built sandcastles and buried their dad in the sand. I would never see or hear that joint laughter again. The sight of Paul playing

with Adam made the emptiness of my heart all the more
intense. Since the onset of Matthew's illness, I had been his
primary carer, so the natural pairing had been Paul and
Adam, and myself and Matthew. Paul still had his playmate.
I didn't.

Christmas was the next hurdle to overcome. Again, the
need to buy Mattie presents was overwhelming. In not buy-
ing his presents, I felt as though I was neglecting him, but
there was no 'him' to neglect. I had always (and still do)
keep Christmas cards from close relatives from the previous
year. In among the Christmas decorations, I found Mattie's
cards. His attempts at writing his name were scrawled
inside. I would never have another card from my son. There
would always be an empty space where his card would
have stood. Also in the box were the decorations he had
made at playschool, still with his name tag on them: a paper
angel and a plastic cup sprayed with glitter and edged with
tinsel. Both of them were put on the Christmas tree that
year and every year thereafter. The angel only lasted five or
six years, but the cup has survived until now!

That first Christmas morning without Mattie was inde-
scribable. Somehow I summoned up some enthusiasm for
Adam's sake, but all I wanted to do was weep. The thought
of spending Christmas Day at home was horrendous, but
we couldn't go away and leave our parents to face Christmas on their own. With both of us being only children, they
had nowhere else to go. So we came to a compromise. After
the Christmas morning service, Paul, Adam and I had lunch
at Kev and Andrea's house, then walked home in time for
our parents' visit in the afternoon.

To me, the end of the year brought finality to life with

Mattie. For nearly five years I had had the benefit of living with and being responsible for a very special little boy. That time had come to an end. But the greater privilege of being his mum would continue throughout my lifetime. Loving him would go beyond life into eternity.

However, facing the New Year was very hard. Most people enter January with hope; I entered it that year with a vacuum in my heart. I still loved Adam very much and did everything for him. I was still very much in love with Paul, even though I couldn't physically love him for several months. Never once in that time did he put pressure on me; he just waited until my deep mourning was over. I still had a fantastic family and I still had to go on living. But how could I, without Mattie?

As I entered the New Year, I had a choice to make. Should I just exist or should I make the most of the rest of my life? Should I live passively or passionately? One of my favourite Bible verses is John 10:10, where Jesus says, 'The thief comes only to steal and kill and destroy; I have come that they may have life, and have it to the full.' My life at that stage was on the point of destruction, but I knew deep within my heart that if I asked Jesus, he would help me to have a full life, despite the loss of Mattie. I was still in mourning and would have to work through a lot more grief, but I believed that if I trusted my Saviour, he would see me through this 'valley of the shadow of death', and I could learn to live again after Matthew. I remembered my promise to Mattie, moments before the undertakers took him away, that his life would not be in vain and that while I had breath his story would be told. If I chose to live passively, then that promise would never be fulfilled. My decision was clear cut. That day, early in January 1987, I chose to live the remainder of my life to the full, to live out my days passionately, not only for myself but for the memory of my son.

All our family believe that Mattie is in heaven with Jesus, his Saviour and Lord, his best Friend. I have always wanted the best for my children and have always put their needs before my own. Regarding Mattie, my need would be to have him here on earth with me, outliving me, but I believe that what he has now and what he is experiencing now far outweighs anything that this life can offer. The two are incomparable. How can I, as his loving mother, wish to pull him away from the amazing experience of heaven (where there is no sorrow, no tears and no death) just for me and my needs? I cannot. I love him too much. Heaven is far better than earth. One day, when my destiny is complete, when I have fulfilled my purpose, then I will have the joy of spending eternity with him. You may ask how I can be so sure. I believe my Bible from cover to cover; I do not pick and choose verses to suit my needs, but I do have some favourite passages; for example, John's Gospel. John chapter 3 explains how we can be sure of a secure future in heaven, and chapter 14 tells us what it's like there.

I would never have chosen the path I trod, but it was far better to have taken every difficult step than never to have 'walked' with Mattie at all. How true is the old saying 'Far better to have loved and lost, than never to have loved at all'! I feel as though I gave a lifetime of love to my son in those four short years. We created precious memories that will last me my whole life. As humans we see a life as being complete after 70 years or more and we consider anything less to be a shortened life span, but I do not believe God sees things in the same light. We live in time, but he lives in eternity. I believe every one of us has a destiny or purpose to fulfil and when that is completed, then life will be over. It takes most people 70 years to reach that point. Mattie accomplished what God required of him in just under five years. His life, in God's eyes, was complete.

The year 1987 was the beginning of a whole new life for me. It was like stepping out into the dark, not knowing what lay ahead. I trusted that the same God who had seen me through the darkest phase of my life would lead me out into the sunshine once again. I had to believe that one day I would be able to look back on that season and trace my journey from tragedy through to triumph.

Epilogue

The dream of writing *Harvest from Heartache* was birthed several years after Matthew's death. The desire to see the dream fulfilled has grown stronger as the years have unfolded, but it has taken two decades for the dream to become a reality. Why has it taken so long? Until now the time was not right and I was not ready. The story would not have been written with the same depth, ten or even five years ago. Do you remember reading the story I told Mattie of the grain of wheat in the farmer's field? Do you remember the view that Mattie had of the field of wheat when he walked alongside it and then how the vista changed when I held him up in my arms? Do you remember reading about the ear of corn he held in his hands and how he looked across the whole field and it was full of them? Well, if I'd written the book any sooner, I would have been writing from a very different perspective. I would have only been reporting on 'an ear' or perhaps 'a sheaf' of corn, certainly not 'a whole wheat field'.

So many amazing things have come out of Matthew's story – too many to be told in this book. The way his journey affected the career Adam chose and how Debbie's (Adam's wife) family's story is closely interwoven with ours is astonishing. The decision Paul and I made to have another child was not taken lightly and there were many disappointments and sorrows to encounter first; the joy of having pregnancies confirmed only to experience the misery of miscarriages was difficult to bear. The sheer panic over a tumour in Adam's throat two years after Mattie's death caused me to 'shake a fist at God' and reassess my motherhood. But finally, our mourning turned into dancing when in August 1989 I gave birth to a delightful baby girl called Bethany. She has become a very beautiful young woman and lives life with a passion that is compelling. God knew what I needed to heal a broken heart!

My father is the sole survivor of our parents. He has reached 85 years of age and is very fit and active. His body may be getting old, but his spirit certainly isn't; he is a great delight to be with as he positively looks to the future.

Matthew's life, and indeed death, changed many things in our personal lives, including our priorities and our careers. Other things became far more important than being successful or wealthy. A sense of destiny rested on our shoulders in a very positive sense. We began to realise that there was more to the journey of dealing with the cancer and death of our child than we initially thought. We are not the same people as we were back then. We are far more understanding and compassionate, much wiser and less judgemental. We have acquired a wealth of life's experiences, which in itself has brought a greater maturity to our lives. However, without our faith I believe our lives would have turned out very differently.

After Matthew's death, the number of people attending our church began to increase. The school was no longer a suitable venue, so in 1990 a modern new church was built with a seating capacity of 240. The number of people has continued to increase and for the last two years we have had to have three services every Sunday in order to accommodate the people who want to attend. We are desperately searching for larger premises once again! Calvary Church is a very modern, evangelistic church, serving the needs of the community. The vast majority are under 40 years of age and literally hundreds of teenagers and 'twenties' attend. Many of our youth workers were Matthew's best friends, including Andrew, or Andy as he is now known. Nicola is still also part of our church, but is doing social work in Manchester.

Our influence has gone way past the geographical boundary of Kingswinford. Paul and I have travelled to four continents incorporating Matthew's story in our seminars and sermons, proving how a person can live again after a major tragedy. This year Calvary Church is planting a new church in Slovakia, training locals to become leaders in their own right. We have sent workers out to Poland, Lanzarote, America, India, South Africa, China and Australia. Pam, my friend whom I introduced to Jesus and who became an amazing support to us, regularly takes teams out to Bosnia to help those who have been devastated by the war and to inspire hope once again.

These are just a few of the stories I could tell of the harvest Matthew's life has brought. So many triumphs have come out of our tragedy, including that of my own life – how the revelation of dark secrets from my own past led to a remarkable change in my life. But that, as they say, is another story.

Finally, as part of my research for this book, Paul and I

went to view Matthew's medical records at both Russell's Hall Hospital and the Birmingham Children's Hospital. I was surprised to find that at the children's hospital there was an order written over his records: 'Never to be Destroyed'. When I asked the reason for this order, I was very surprised at the reply: 'Well, Mrs Chamberlain, your son has given life to other children. His records are invaluable to medical research. They will be kept here for 50 years and then transferred to the UK Medical Archives for ever. Matthew's records will be used beyond your lifetime. In a sense, he will live on after you.' What a legacy our darling son has left behind! A harvest truly has, and still is, being produced from our years of heartache.

Resources and Contacts

If you have been affected by any issues raised in this book and would like to speak to someone, please feel free to make contact with any of these organisations who would be more than happy to offer help.

Care for the Family

The Bereaved Parents' Network is part of Care for the Family, a charity which has been supporting and encouraging families since 1988.

Care for the Family
Garth House
Leon Avenue
Cardiff CF15 7RG
Tel: (029) 2081 1733
Fax: (029) 2081 4089
Email: mail@cff.org.uk
www.careforthefamily.org.uk/bpn

Alpha

For more information on the Christian faith, Alpha will point you in the direction of a local Alpha course, where you can ask as many questions as you like in a non-threatening environment.

The Alpha Office
Holy Trinity Brompton
Brompton Road
London SW7 1JA
Tel: (020) 7052 0274
Email: info@alphacourse.org.uk
www.alpha.org.uk

UCB

For a confidential prayer line (not a counselling or advice service):
UCB Prayerline
Tel: 0845 456 7729 (Mon – Fri 9.00am – 10.30pm)
Text: PRAY <your requestM\#62> to 80377

Birmingham Children's Hospital

If you feel you would like to make a donation to help those children who are receiving treatment for all cancers, including leukaemia, then please make cheques payable to Birmingham Children's Charities (specifying the Oncology Department) and citing this book as a reference.

Fund-Raising Department
Birmingham Children's Hospital
Steelhouse Lane
Birmingham B4 6NH
Tel: (0121) 333 8502
Email: webmaster@bch.nhs.org.uk

www.bch.org.uk

(Registered Charity No. 1074850)

Leukaemia Research Fund

The leading national charity for research into all forms of leukaemia, lymphoma and related cancers of the blood, they also operate a helpful information service.

If you feel you would like to make a donation towards research for a cure, then make cheques payable to Leukaemia Research Fund.

Leukaemia Research Fund

43 Great Ormond Street

London

WC1N 3JJ

Tel: (020) 7405 0101

Email: info@lrf.org.uk

www.lrf.org.uk

(Registered Charity No. 216032)

The Shaming of the Strong

by Sarah Williams

She was going to be a mum again, and the whole family's excitement was growing day by day.

But the hospital scan changed everything.

'To be pregnant with a much longed for child is a joyful experience for most women. But if you know that this baby is so grossly deformed that she cannot be born alive – what then? Do you carry her tenderly to term and love her while you can, or do you terminate a life that is, in the eyes of the medical profession, of no worth? In this heartwrenchingly honest book, SarahWilliams and her husband face these issues with shining faith and courage that challenge us all to reconsider what we value and to understand more clearly what is precious to the heart of God.'

Marion Stoud

SARAH WILLIAMS is an Associate Professor of Church History at Regent College, Vancouver and until recently was a history tutor at Lincoln College, Oxford. She is married to Paul and lives in Canada with her two daughters Hannah and Emilia. She is the daughter of Jennifer Rees Larcombe.

 www.kingsway.co.uk